ABOUT THE AUTHORS

Each of the authors brings a wealth of past experiences to the Basic Math program at Camden County College and through their combined efforts they have created a comprehensive review text to be used with any computation course.

Ellen Freedman earned a B.S. in Mathematics Education at Temple University and an M.A. in Learning Disabilities at Rowan College of New Jersey. Ellen taught high school mathematics in Philadelphia, and worked in industry as a computer systems analyst before settling in at Camden County College. She has taught basic skills mathematics at the college since 1988, including special sections for students with learning disabilities. She has given regional and national workshops on math anxiety, learning styles, teaching mathematics to college students with learning disabilities and how to incorporate technology and the Internet into the math classroom. She has won national awards for her use of multimedia and technology in the classroom. Ellen's math anxiety web site, www.mathpower.com has received numerous awards and is recommended by the The National Council of Teachers of Mathematics, The Australian Association of Mathematics Teachers and the Canadian Mathematical Society.

Kelly Jackson graduated from Franklin and Marshall College with a B.A. degree in Mathematics. She holds a Master's Degree in Community College Teaching with a Specialization in Mathematics from Rowan University and a Master's Degree in Educational Studies from the University of Delaware. She is currently ABD at the University of Delaware for a PhD in Measurement, Statistics and Evaluation. Kelly was hired as a fulltime faculty member in 1992. She is an Associate Professor, with a dual appointment in the Math Department and the Basic Skills Math Department. She is currently the chair of the Basic Skills Math Department. Kelly speaks regularly at workshops and conferences on topics such as: teaching math to students with learning disabilities, using the TI-83 calculator in a statistics classroom, and teaching math to students with hearing loss. She is fluent in American Sign Language, and teaches all of the developmental math courses offered at the Mid-Atlantic Post Secondary Center for the Deaf and Hard of Hearing, which is housed at the college.

Virginia Licata received a B.A. in Mathematics from St. Bonaventure University and an MATM from Villanova University. Ginny taught in high schools in Florida, New Jersey and New York from 1961 to 1980 when she joined Camden County College as Coordinator of Basic Math Skills. From 1986 to 1988, she also coordinated a large Challenge Grant, and during that time passing and retention rates in the math classrooms increased and a calculator experiment was introduced. Ginny is active in the Mathematics Association of Two Year Colleges of New Jersey, and she was an original member of the New Jersey Basic Skills Math Advisory Committee. In January of 1992 Ginny joined the ranks of Camden County College's Basic Skills Math faculty and served as the first chairman of the Math Skills Department.

Barbara Jane Sparks holds an A.A. from Salem Community College, a B.A. in Mathematics and a M.A. in Community College Education from Glassboro State College. In 1990 she joined Camden County College as the first full-time faculty member in the Basic Skills Math Program. During her twenty-one years as a full-time developmental mathematics instructor, she has taught at two New Jersey Community Colleges and at the University of Delaware. As a former non-traditional community college student, BJ is familiar with the academic needs of the adult learner. She has developed many unique and interesting ways to approach some of the more difficult topics in developmental mathematics, and continues to share her ideas with her students and colleagues through various workshops at the local and national level.

Preface

Math Fundamentals—A Review is a workbook designed for use in any math basic skills course. A student can retrace typical arithmetic problems to review basic numerical processes and practice business and consumer applications, percents, statistics, geometry, and conversion. Upon completion of these review exercises, the student should be prepared to take any entrance test or placement test involving basic math skills.

This book is a pool of carefully sequenced problems for students to use when preparing for unit or cumulative tests (such as final exams). Each of the nine units contains at least two free response forms and a multiple choice form. There is also a comprehensive review with problems from all nine units. Answers are provided for all problems in this workbook.

Contents

Math Fundamentals Review

Unit 1

Whole Numbers

Review Form A

1. Place the correct symbol, < or >, between the two numbers.

    a. a. 6 __ 8   b. 5 __ 0

2. Write 342,506 in words: _____

3. Write two million two hundred two thousand two in standard form.   _____

4. Round 456,817 to the nearest:

    a. Ten-thousands _____ b. Hundreds _____ c. Thousands _____

5. Round 34,907 to the nearest:

    a. Thousands _____   b. Tens _____   c. Ten-thousands _____

Perform the indicated operations:

6. $305 + 5,602 + 24$ 7. $1,807 - 898$

8. $5,029 \bullet 78$ 9. $13,802 \div 15$

10. $16 - 4 + 8$ 11. $20 + 4^2 \div 2$

12. $14 + 7 \div 7$ 13. $24 \div 4 - 2^2$

14. $(10 - 8)^3 - 12 \div 3 \bullet 2 + 1$ 15. $16 - 4 \div 2 + 3^2 - (8 - 5)$

16.   Write the expression in exponential notation: $2 \bullet 2 \bullet 2 \bullet 2 \bullet 3 \bullet 3$

17. Find the value of: a. 12 decreased by 5   b. the product of 3 and 16

18. Which problem has an answer of 0?   a. $0 \div 8$ b. $8 \div 0$

Translate and solve the word problems:

19. As an investment, Richard bought four hundred nine shares of stock at $58 per share. How much did he spend on all the stock?

20. Amber's credit card had a balance of $847 before she went shopping. If she used her credit card to charge a dress for $49, a pair of shoes for $38, and some jewelry for $27, how much does she now owe on her credit card?

21. Eileen earns $36,408 annually. How much does she earn each month?

22. Heather's financial award for school this semester is $2,400. If she pays $2,100 in tuition, $62 for her science book, $48 for her psychology book, $39 for her math book, and $55 for her English book, how much money will she have left for her art supplies?

23. Which is more, $3825 divided between three people or $2548 divided between two people?

24. David picked 200 pounds of tomatoes on Monday and 248 pounds of tomatoes on Tuesday.

    a. If he packs 4 pounds of tomatoes in a box, how many boxes will he have to sell?
    b. If he gets $3 a dollar a box, how much did he earn from the tomatoes?

25. Find the **perimeter** of the following figures:

a.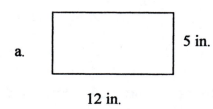

5 in.

12 in.

b.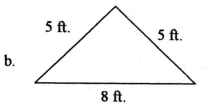

5 ft.

5 ft.

8 ft.

26. Find the **area** of the given figures:

a.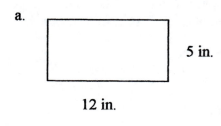

5 in.

12 in.

b.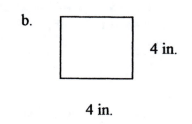

4 in.

4 in.

Unit 1

Review Form B

1. Place the correct symbol, < or >, between the two numbers.

   a. 9 __ 3

   b. 0 __ 1

2. Write 516,428 in words. ─────────────────────────

3. Write two hundred twenty-four thousand sixty-two in standard form. ──────────

4. Round 58,426 to the nearest:

   a. Ten-thousands ─────── b. Hundreds ─────── c. Thousands ───────

5. Round 149,426 to the nearest:

   a. Hundred-thousands ─────── b. Tens ─────── c. Thousands ───────

Perform the indicated operations:

6. $24 + 1,509 + 287$

7. $2,083 - 984$

8. $(3,708)(69)$

9. $2,544 \div 24$

10. $24 - 4 + 2$

11. $10 - 4 \div 2$

12. $18 + 9 \div 9$

13. $200 \div 5 - 5^2$

14. $2^3 \div (5 - 3)^2$

15. $21 - 12 \div 3 + 2 \bullet (4 - 1)$

16. Write in exponential notation: $2 \cdot 2 \cdot 5 \cdot 5 \cdot 5 \cdot 5 \cdot 7 \cdot 7 \cdot 7$

17. Find the value of: a. 12 subtracted from 15   b. the quotient of 15 and 3

18. Which problem has an answer of 0?   a. $6 \div 0$ b. $0 \div 6$

Translate and solve the word problems:

19. John had $847 in his checkbook. He wrote checks to pay $126 on his charge card, $98 for new tires and $59 to his doctor. How much is left in his checkbook?

20. Sixteen Camden County College employees shared the winning ticket for the $1,500,000 lottery prize. How much did each employee win?

21. Kelly bought nine suits, which were $137 each. How much did she spend?

22. Bob's tires had a 50,000-mile warranty on them. If he has driven 37,879 miles, how many miles are left on the warranty?

23. Richard's car expenses for the year included $4612 for loan payments, $2857 for gas, $1628 of insurance, and $635 for maintenance.

    a. What was his total car expense for the year?

    b. What did his car expense average per month?

24. Sandy's new car cost $16,872. She took out a three-year loan with a monthly payment of $528.

    a. How much did she pay through her loan in three years?

    b. How much more did she pay than the cost of the car?

25. Find the **perimeter** of the following figures:

a.  5 ft.

14 ft.

b.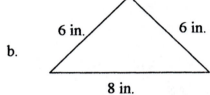

6 in.   6 in.

8 in.

26. Find the **area** of the given figures:

a. 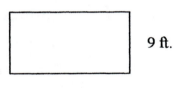 9 ft.

16 ft.

 3 in.

3 in.

Unit 1

Multiple Choice Review Form C

1. Which statement is correct?

   a. $6 > 9$ b. $7 < 4$ c. $5 > 1$ d. $9 < 0$

2. Write three hundred eighty-two thousand four hundred twenty-six in standard form.

   a. 3,820,426   b. 300,820,426   c. 382,426   d. 382,400,026

3. Round 364,784 off to the nearest ten thousand.

   a. 400,000   b. 360,000   c. 364,000   d. 360,700

4. Add: $1,267 + 789 + 94$

   a. 2,159   b. 2,140   c. 2,150   d. 2,149

5. Subtract: $1,098 - 389$

   a. 719   b. 709   c. 609   d. 1,487

6. Multiply: $(397)(68)$

   a. 26,928   b. 26,316   c. 26,988   d. 26,996

7. Divide: $57\overline{)5,913}$

   a. 101 r 56   b. 103 r 42   c. 104 r 2   d. 13 r 42

8. Simplify: $9 - 3(4-2) \div 3 + 5$

   a. 9   b. 6   c. 12   d. 2

9. Write the prime factorization of 72 in exponential form.

   a. $3^2 \bullet 2^2$ b. $9 \bullet 2^3$ c. $3^2 \bullet 2^3$ d. $3^3 \bullet 2^2$

10. A jeweler has twenty-eight ounces of gold made into 4-ounce gold bars. The gold bars are then sold for $1,089 each. How much money did the jeweler get for selling all the gold bars he made?

    a. $7,623   b. $8,712   c. $7,614   d. $7,603

1. Ginny earned $15 on Monday, $27 on Tuesday, $34 on Wednesday, and $46 on Thursday. What is the total that she earned for the week?

2. Bob had $2,105 in his savings account. He withdrew $1,987. How much is left in his account?

3. Sue's car gets 32 miles per gallon. How far can she travel on 12 gallons of gas?

4. Richard bought a new 52-inch television/stereo system for $2,450. He paid $98 a month in payments. How many months did it take for him to pay for the television?

5. Catherine has been saving $30 per week for the past two years to buy a used car. The used car she wants costs $3,250. Does she have enough money to buy the car?

6. David had $738 in his checkbook. He deposited $1,267 into his account. He then wrote a check for $1,986. How much is left in the checkbook?

7. Dorothy picked 60 pounds of apples and Kelly picked 64 pounds of apples. They then packaged their apples in containers that held 4 pounds each. How many 4-pound containers did they have?

8. Betty earns $420 for a forty-hour week. She also gets $13 per hour for any overtime she works. How much does she earn in a week where she works 59 hours?

9. John drove at 65 miles per hour on the turnpike. How many hours had John been driving after he had traveled 780 miles?

10. Martha can make fifteen ties an hour. At the end of the day, she then packs 24 ties per box for shipping. How many boxes can she ship in an eight-hour workday?

Answers to Unit 1, Review Form A

1. a. <   b. >

2. Three hundred forty-two thousand, five hundred six

3. 2,202,002

4. a. 460 000

   b. 456,800

   c. 457,000

5. a. 35,000

   b. 34,910

   c. 30,000

6. 5,931

7. 909

8. 392,262

9. 920 r 2

10. 20

11. 28

12. 15

13. 2

14. 1

15. 20

16. $2^4 \cdot 3^2$

17. a. 7

    b. 48

18. a.

19. $23,722

20. $961

21. $3,034

22. $96

23. $3,825 by 3 people

24. a. 112 boxes   b. $336

25. a. 34 in.   b. 18 ft.

26. a. 60 sq. in.   b. 16 sq. in.

Answer to Unit 1, Review Form B

1. a. >   b. <

2. Five hundred sixteen thousand, four hundred twenty-eight

3. 224,062

4. a. 60,000

   b. 58,430

   c. 58,000

5. a. 100,000

   b. 149,430

   c. 149,000

6. 1,820

7. 1,099

8. 255,852

9. 106

10. 22

11. 8

12. 19

13. 15

14. 2

15. 23

16. $2^2 \cdot 5^4 \cdot 7^3$

17. a. 3

    b. 5

18. b

19. $564

20. $93,750

21. $1,233

22. 12,121 miles

23. a. $9,732   b. $811

24. a. $19,008   b. $2,136

25. a. 38 ft.   b. 20 in.

26. a. 144 sq. ft.   b. 9 sq. in.

Answers to Unit 1, Multiple Choice Review Form C

1. c

2. c

3. b

4. c

5. b

6. d

7. b

8. c

9. c

10. a

Answer to Unit 1, Review Form D

1. $122

2. $118

3. 384 miles

4. 25 months

5. NO

6. $19

7. 31

8. $667

9. 12 hours

10. 5 boxes

Math Fundamentals Review

Unit 2

Fractions

Unit 2

Review Form A

1. List **all** the factors of: a. 48   b. 36   c. 81

2. Find the **prime** factorization of: a. 36   b. 81   c. 54

3. Find the **GCF** of   a. 32 and 48   b. 18 and 27

4. Express the shaded portion of the boxes as an **improper fraction** and as a **mixed number**.

 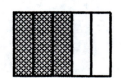

5. Convert the following improper fractions into **mixed numbers**.

     a. $\dfrac{25}{6}$ b. $\dfrac{17}{3}$ c. $\dfrac{39}{7}$ d. $\dfrac{47}{8}$ e. $\dfrac{59}{5}$

6. Convert the following mixed numbers into **improper fractions**.

     a. $1\dfrac{7}{9}$ b. $2\dfrac{5}{9}$ c. $5\dfrac{1}{6}$ d. $7\dfrac{2}{3}$ e. $3\dfrac{4}{5}$

7. Build an equivalent fraction for:

     a. $\dfrac{2}{3} = \dfrac{?}{12}$ b. $\dfrac{5}{6} = \dfrac{15}{?}$ c. $\dfrac{5}{9} = \dfrac{?}{36}$ d. $\dfrac{5}{7} = \dfrac{30}{?}$

8. Simplify the fractions to lowest terms.

     a. $\dfrac{8}{12}$ b. $\dfrac{15}{24}$ c. $\dfrac{22}{33}$ d. $\dfrac{25}{60}$ e. $\dfrac{40}{1000}$

9. Multiply: a. $\dfrac{16}{25} \bullet \dfrac{5}{24}$ b. $\dfrac{13}{15} \bullet \dfrac{35}{39}$ c. $\dfrac{5}{6} \bullet 30$ d. $\dfrac{51}{52} \bullet \dfrac{4}{9}$

10. Multiply: a. $2\dfrac{2}{3} \bullet 6\dfrac{3}{4}$ b. $\left(3\dfrac{3}{4}\right)\left(8\dfrac{2}{5}\right)$ c. $\left(1\dfrac{5}{6}\right)\left(2\dfrac{2}{5}\right)$ d. $12 \bullet 2\dfrac{1}{3}$

11. Divide: a. $\dfrac{2}{3} \div \dfrac{1}{2}$ b. $16 \div \dfrac{1}{2}$ c. $\dfrac{8}{15} \div \dfrac{10}{24}$ d. $\dfrac{5}{6} \div 15$

12. Divide: a. $5\dfrac{1}{4} \div \dfrac{3}{8}$ b. $16 \div 2\dfrac{2}{3}$ c. $6\dfrac{3}{7} \div 2\dfrac{1}{2}$ d. $3\dfrac{3}{8} \div 9$

13. Simplify: a. $\dfrac{\frac{2}{3}}{4}$ b. $\dfrac{\frac{3}{4}}{\frac{1}{2}}$ c. $\dfrac{6}{\frac{2}{3}}$ d. $\dfrac{\frac{5}{8}}{\frac{1}{4}}$

14. Find the LCM of :
   a. 6 and 9   b. 18 and 24   c. 15 and 25   d. 6, 8 and 9

15. Place the correct symbol, < or > , between the two numbers.

   a. $\dfrac{5}{6} \quad \dfrac{7}{9}$ b. $\dfrac{3}{5} \quad \dfrac{15}{22}$ c. $\dfrac{7}{15} \quad \dfrac{13}{24}$

16. Add: a. $\dfrac{5}{6} + \dfrac{2}{3}$ b. $\dfrac{5}{12} + \dfrac{7}{16}$ c. $\dfrac{7}{9} + \dfrac{8}{15}$ d. $\dfrac{3}{8} + \dfrac{5}{10}$

17. Add: a. $\begin{array}{r} 2\frac{7}{16} \\ + 8\frac{7}{12} \\ \hline \end{array}$ b. $\begin{array}{r} 3\frac{2}{3} \\ + 4\frac{5}{8} \\ \hline \end{array}$ c. $\begin{array}{r} 14\frac{5}{12} \\ + 11\frac{7}{16} \\ \hline \end{array}$ d. $\begin{array}{r} 9\frac{4}{15} \\ + 3\frac{3}{20} \\ \hline \end{array}$

18. Subtract: a. $\dfrac{8}{9} - \dfrac{3}{4}$ b. $\dfrac{11}{12} - \dfrac{2}{3}$ c. $\dfrac{9}{16} - \dfrac{1}{3}$ d. $\dfrac{4}{5} - \dfrac{5}{8}$

19. Subtract: a. $\begin{array}{r} 8\frac{5}{6} \\ -\ 3\frac{2}{3} \\ \hline \end{array}$ b. $\begin{array}{r} 8\frac{1}{4} \\ -\ 2 \\ \hline \end{array}$ c. $\begin{array}{r} 7 \\ -\ 2\frac{3}{5} \\ \hline \end{array}$ d. $\begin{array}{r} 5\frac{1}{6} \\ -\ 4\frac{5}{6} \\ \hline \end{array}$

20. Subtract: a. $\begin{array}{r} 8\frac{1}{6} \\ -\ 3\frac{2}{3} \\ \hline \end{array}$ b. $\begin{array}{r} 3\frac{2}{5} \\ -\ 1\frac{7}{10} \\ \hline \end{array}$ c. $\begin{array}{r} 9 \\ -\ 7\frac{7}{8} \\ \hline \end{array}$ d. $\begin{array}{r} 21\frac{2}{5} \\ -\ 15\frac{3}{7} \\ \hline \end{array}$

21. Simplify: a. $\dfrac{3}{4} - \dfrac{1}{3} \cdot \dfrac{1}{2}$ b. $\dfrac{5}{6} - \dfrac{3}{4} + \dfrac{1}{8}$ c. $\dfrac{5}{8} \div \dfrac{1}{2} \cdot \dfrac{1}{4}$

22. Simplify: a. $\left(\dfrac{2}{3}\right)^3 \cdot \left(\dfrac{3}{4}\right)^2$ b. $\dfrac{3}{4} - \left(\dfrac{1}{2}\right)^2 \cdot \dfrac{3}{5}$ c. $\left(\dfrac{5}{9} - \dfrac{1}{18}\right)^3 + \dfrac{1}{6} \div \dfrac{2}{3}$

23. Richard bought a share of stock for $\$48\frac{1}{4}$ on Monday. It gained $1\frac{1}{2}$ on Tuesday, but lost $\frac{3}{8}$ on Wednesday. What is the current value of the stock?

24. How many $\dfrac{3}{4}$ ounce servings of cereal are contained within a 15-ounce box of cereal?

25. On a recent diet, Sue lost $6\frac{1}{2}$ pounds the first week, $3\frac{1}{4}$ pounds the second week, and $5\frac{1}{8}$ pounds the third week. How many pounds has Sue lost in three weeks?

26. The farmer sold $5\frac{1}{2}$ acres for \$88,000. How much money did he get per acre?

27. The party favors require $\frac{3}{4}$ of a yard of lace and $\frac{3}{8}$ yard of pearls.

    a. How many yards of lace are required for sixteen party favors?

    b. How many party favors can be made from 15 yards of pearls?

28. If Joe spends $\frac{1}{3}$ of his income on rent and $\frac{1}{4}$ of his income on food, what fractional partion of his money is left?

29. If Steve plants $\frac{1}{3}$ of his garden in corn, and $\frac{3}{8}$ of his garden in tomatoes, what fractional partion of his garden is left to plant other vegetables?

30. Find the **perimeter and area** of the following figures:

a.
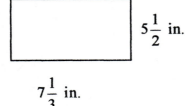
$5\frac{1}{2}$ in.

$7\frac{1}{3}$ in.

b.
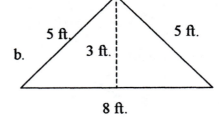
5 ft. 3 ft. 5 ft.

8 ft.

c.
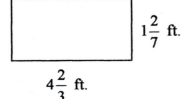
$1\frac{2}{7}$ ft.

$4\frac{2}{3}$ ft.

d.
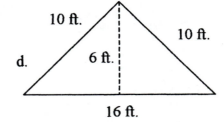
10 ft. 6 ft. 10 ft.

16 ft.

Unit 2

Review Form B

1. List **all** the factors of :   a. 24   b. 72   c. 51

2. Find the **prime factorization** of: a. 72   b. 48   d. 64

3. Find the GCF of: a. 24 and 36   b. 16 and 48

4. Express the shaded boxes as a **mixed number** and as an **improper fraction**.

  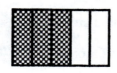

5. Convert the following improper fractions into **mixed numbers**.

    a. $\dfrac{32}{5}$ b. $\dfrac{17}{2}$ c. $\dfrac{45}{7}$ d. $\dfrac{55}{10}$ e. $\dfrac{27}{4}$

6. Convert the following mixed numbers into **improper fractions**.

    a. $5\dfrac{3}{4}$ b. $4\dfrac{2}{3}$ c. $6\dfrac{3}{5}$ d. $7\dfrac{3}{8}$ e. $3\dfrac{2}{5}$

7. Build an equivalent fraction for:

    a. $\dfrac{2}{3}=\dfrac{?}{27}$ b. $\dfrac{5}{6}=\dfrac{20}{?}$ c. $\dfrac{5}{9}=\dfrac{?}{45}$ d. $\dfrac{5}{7}=\dfrac{45}{?}$

8. Simplify the following to lowest terms:

    a. $\dfrac{12}{18}$ b. $\dfrac{15}{27}$ c. $\dfrac{22}{55}$ d. $\dfrac{25}{35}$ e. $\dfrac{60}{1000}$

9. Multiply: a. $\dfrac{13}{24}\bullet\dfrac{9}{26}$ b. $\dfrac{22}{25}\bullet\dfrac{5}{11}$ c. $\dfrac{21}{50}\bullet\dfrac{25}{48}$ d. $40\bullet\dfrac{5}{8}$

10. Multiply: a. $2\dfrac{1}{10} \bullet 3\dfrac{3}{4}$ b. $\left(2\dfrac{1}{4}\right)\left(5\dfrac{1}{3}\right)$ c. $\left(6\dfrac{1}{4}\right)\left(2\dfrac{2}{5}\right)$ d. $2\dfrac{1}{6} \bullet 3$

11. Divide: a. $\dfrac{12}{25} \div \dfrac{32}{15}$ b. $24 \div \dfrac{1}{2}$ c. $\dfrac{7}{15} \div \dfrac{21}{25}$ d. $\dfrac{2}{3} \div 6$

12. Divide: a. $2\dfrac{5}{8} \div 1\dfrac{1}{5}$ b. $4\dfrac{3}{8} \div 5$ c. $5\dfrac{1}{4} \div 3\dfrac{1}{2}$ d. $\dfrac{5}{9} \div 45$

13. Simplify: a. $\dfrac{\frac{3}{4}}{12}$ b. $\dfrac{\frac{5}{6}}{\frac{2}{3}}$ c. $\dfrac{12}{\frac{2}{3}}$ d. $\dfrac{\frac{3}{8}}{\frac{3}{4}}$

14. Find the **LCM** of:

   a. 8 and 12   b. 30 and 12   c. 16 and 24   d. 4, 6, and 9

15. Place the correct symbol, $<$ or $>$, between the two numbers.

   a. $\dfrac{10}{13}$ $\dfrac{5}{8}$ b. $\dfrac{2}{3}$ $\dfrac{13}{15}$ c. $\dfrac{4}{15}$ $\dfrac{7}{18}$

16. Add: a. $\dfrac{4}{27} + \dfrac{5}{18}$ b. $\dfrac{5}{7} + \dfrac{11}{21}$ c. $\dfrac{9}{10} + \dfrac{7}{15}$ d. $\dfrac{11}{30} + \dfrac{7}{45}$

17. Add: a. $\begin{aligned}3\dfrac{5}{12}\\ +\,2\dfrac{7}{9}\\ \hline\end{aligned}$ b. $\begin{aligned}4\dfrac{1}{3}\\ +\,5\dfrac{5}{7}\\ \hline\end{aligned}$ c. $\begin{aligned}8\dfrac{11}{15}\\ +\,3\dfrac{8}{25}\\ \hline\end{aligned}$ d. $\begin{aligned}8\dfrac{5}{8}\\ +\,1\dfrac{1}{6}\\ \hline\end{aligned}$

18. Subtract: a. $\dfrac{7}{15} - \dfrac{3}{20}$ b. $\dfrac{11}{15} - \dfrac{2}{3}$ c. $\dfrac{7}{12} - \dfrac{1}{3}$ d. $\dfrac{11}{24} - \dfrac{5}{32}$

19. Subtract: a. $\begin{array}{r} 9\frac{3}{4} \\ -\,5\frac{1}{2} \\ \hline \end{array}$ b. $\begin{array}{r} 9\frac{1}{7} \\ -\,6 \\ \hline \end{array}$ c. $\begin{array}{r} 5\frac{1}{3} \\ -\,2\frac{2}{3} \\ \hline \end{array}$ d. $\begin{array}{r} 6 \\ -\,2\frac{5}{11} \\ \hline \end{array}$

20. Subtract: a. $\begin{array}{r} 15\frac{1}{6} \\ -\,9\frac{2}{3} \\ \hline \end{array}$ b. $\begin{array}{r} 16\frac{1}{8} \\ -\,9\frac{5}{6} \\ \hline \end{array}$ c. $\begin{array}{r} 8\frac{7}{10} \\ -\,7\frac{9}{10} \\ \hline \end{array}$ d. $\begin{array}{r} 9\frac{7}{12} \\ -\,4\frac{7}{8} \\ \hline \end{array}$

21. Simplify: a. $\dfrac{7}{8} - \dfrac{1}{2} + \dfrac{1}{4}$ b. $\dfrac{11}{12} \div \dfrac{3}{4} \bullet \dfrac{1}{3}$ c. $\dfrac{3}{4} + \dfrac{1}{4} \bullet \dfrac{2}{3}$

22. Simplify: a. $\left(\dfrac{5}{6}\right)^3 \bullet \left(\dfrac{3}{10}\right)^2$ b. $\left(\dfrac{3}{8}\right) + \left(\dfrac{2}{3}\right)^2 \div \dfrac{8}{9}$ c. $\dfrac{5}{12} - \left(\dfrac{3}{5} - \dfrac{1}{2}\right) \bullet \dfrac{5}{6}$

23. A punch recipe calls for $4\frac{2}{3}$ cups of fruit juice, $2\frac{1}{2}$ cups of soda, $\frac{3}{4}$ cup sherbet, and $\frac{1}{8}$ a cup of liquor. How many total cups of ingredients are used in the recipe?

24. How many $\dfrac{3}{4}$ cup sugar bowls can you fill with 48 cups of sugar?

25. A side of beef weighs $186\frac{1}{4}$ pounds. If $48\frac{3}{8}$ pounds of fat and bone are trimmed from the meat, how many pounds of meat are left?

26. An oak tree has been cut up for firewood. If Sue has 36 logs, each of which measure $1\frac{1}{2}$ feet long, how tall was the tree?

27. A pair of shorts requires $\frac{3}{8}$ of a yard of material.

   a. How many yards of material are required for sixteen pair of shorts?

   b. How much will the material cost if it is three and one half-dollars per yard?

28. If John plants $\frac{1}{4}$ of his garden in corn, and $\frac{3}{8}$ of his garden in tomatoes, what fractional partion of his garden is left to plant other vegetables?

29. Aunt Ruby willed $\frac{1}{4}$ of her money to Jane, and $\frac{3}{5}$ of her money to Janelle. The rest of her money is left to you. What fractional partion of her money is left to you?

30. Find the **perimeter and area** of the following figures:

a.

$2\frac{1}{2}$ in.

$5\frac{1}{4}$ in.

b.

9 ft.

27 ft.

9 ft.

c.

$1\frac{2}{3}$ ft.

$3\frac{2}{3}$ ft.

d.

9 ft.

8 ft.

$1\frac{1}{2}$ ft.

8 ft.

21

Multiple Choice Review Form C

1. Which fraction is **_NOT_** equivalent to $\frac{3}{4}$?

   a. $\frac{9}{12}$ b. $\frac{21}{32}$ c. $\frac{15}{20}$ d. $\frac{27}{36}$

2. Add: $\begin{array}{r} 3\frac{7}{16} \\ + 2\frac{7}{12} \\ \hline \end{array}$

   a. $5\frac{1}{2}$ b. $5\frac{1}{48}$ c. $5\frac{35}{48}$ d. $6\frac{1}{48}$

3. Subtract: $\begin{array}{r} 5\frac{5}{12} \\ - 3\frac{3}{5} \\ \hline \end{array}$

   a. $2\frac{11}{60}$ b. $2\frac{49}{60}$ c. $1\frac{49}{60}$ d. $9\frac{1}{60}$

4. Multiply: $\left(5\frac{1}{3}\right)\left(2\frac{1}{16}\right)$

   a. 11 b. $10\frac{1}{48}$ c. $10\frac{1}{24}$ d. $10\frac{5}{16}$

5. Divide: $6\frac{3}{5} \div 2\frac{1}{10}$

   a. $3\frac{3}{5}$ b. $3\frac{1}{7}$ c. $7\frac{6}{7}$ d. $13\frac{43}{50}$

6. Simplify: $\dfrac{5}{6} - \left(\dfrac{2}{3}\right)^2 \bullet \dfrac{3}{8}$

    a. $\dfrac{7}{12}$ b. $\dfrac{1}{8}$ c. $\dfrac{7}{48}$ d. $\dfrac{2}{3}$

7. Simplify: $\dfrac{5}{8} \div \left(\dfrac{2}{3} - \dfrac{1}{4}\right) + \dfrac{5}{6}$

    a. $2\dfrac{1}{3}$ b. $\dfrac{1}{2}$ c. $1\dfrac{1}{8}$ d. $\dfrac{3}{4}$

8. The roofing shingles weigh $78\dfrac{3}{4}$ pounds per bundle. How much does $5\dfrac{3}{5}$ bundles weigh?

    a. 4410 lbs.   b. $73\dfrac{3}{20}$ lbs.   c. $14\dfrac{1}{16}$ lbs.   d. 441 lbs.

9. David drove $151\dfrac{7}{10}$ miles on Monday and $223\dfrac{3}{10}$ miles on Tuesday. If he gets $27\dfrac{1}{2}$ miles per gallon, how many gallons of gas did he use?

    a. $13\dfrac{7}{11}$ gal.   b. $401\dfrac{1}{2}$ gal.   c. $10,321\dfrac{1}{2}$ gal.   d. 150 gal.

10. The movie company's stock was purchased at $\$23\dfrac{1}{2}$. During the first quarter it rose $\$15\dfrac{1}{8}$, but during the second quarter it lost $\$9\dfrac{3}{4}$. How much is the stock now worth?

    a. $\$29\dfrac{1}{8}$ b. $\$48\dfrac{3}{8}$ c. $\$28\dfrac{7}{8}$ d. $\$39\dfrac{7}{8}$

Unit 2

Review Form D

1. Mark ran $2\frac{1}{2}$ miles on Friday, $3\frac{1}{4}$ miles on Saturday, and $2\frac{1}{8}$ miles on Sunday. How many miles did he run in the three days?

2. Georgia bought $7\frac{1}{8}$ pounds of chicken for the barbecue. After removing the skin and bones from the chicken, she only had $5\frac{3}{4}$ pounds of meat left. How many pounds of waste did she have?

3. The plane can hold 232 passengers. If it is $\frac{3}{4}$ full, how many people are on the plane?

4. Jane received $12,600 from Grandpop's estate. If this is $\frac{1}{8}$ of the estate, how much was the entire estate worth?

5. David measured 49 inches tall at the end of the school year. If he had measured $47\frac{1}{4}$ inches at the beginning of the school year, how much had he grown during the year?

6. Nicole's new car gets 27 miles per gallon. How far can she travel on $5\frac{1}{3}$ gallons of gas?

7. Joe planted $\frac{1}{3}$ of his garden in corn, $\frac{1}{8}$ of the garden in sweet potatoes, and $\frac{1}{4}$ of the garden in tomatoes. How much of the garden is <u>left</u> to plant in pumpkins?

8. Richard worked $4\frac{1}{2}$ hours on Monday, $7\frac{1}{3}$ hours on Tuesday, and $5\frac{1}{4}$ on Wednesday. If he is paid $12 an hour, how much money did he earn in the three days?

9. Heather paid $156,000 for $6\frac{1}{2}$ acres of land for a housing development. She set aside $1\frac{1}{4}$ acres for a playground.

    a. How much did she pay per acre?

    b. How many acres were left to build houses on?

10. Brooke picked $11\frac{1}{4}$ pounds of cherries in the morning and $12\frac{1}{2}$ pounds of cherries in the afternoon. She then packaged them in $1\frac{1}{4}$ pound packages to sell.

    a. How many packages did she have to sell that day?

    b. If she received $1\frac{1}{2}$ dollars per package, how much did she earn that day?

Answers to Unit 2, Review Form A

1. a. {1,2,3,4,6,8,12,16,24,48}
   b. {1,2,3,4,6,9,12,18,36}
   c. {1,3,9,27,81}

2. a. $2^2 \cdot 3^2$
   b. 3^4
   c. $3^3 \cdot 2$

3. a. 16   b. 9

4. $\dfrac{8}{5}$ and $1\dfrac{3}{5}$

5.
   a. $4\dfrac{1}{6}$ b. $5\dfrac{2}{3}$ c. $5\dfrac{4}{7}$
   d. $5\dfrac{7}{8}$ e. $11\dfrac{4}{5}$

6.
   a. $\dfrac{16}{9}$ b. $\dfrac{23}{9}$ c. $\dfrac{31}{6}$
   d. $\dfrac{23}{3}$ e. $\dfrac{19}{5}$

7.
   a. $\dfrac{2}{3} = \dfrac{8}{12}$ b. $\dfrac{5}{6} = \dfrac{15}{18}$
   c. $\dfrac{5}{9} = \dfrac{20}{36}$ d. $\dfrac{5}{7} = \dfrac{30}{42}$

8.
   a. $\dfrac{2}{3}$ b. $\dfrac{5}{8}$ c. $\dfrac{2}{3}$
   d. $\dfrac{5}{12}$ e. $\dfrac{1}{25}$

9. a. $\dfrac{2}{15}$ b. $\dfrac{7}{9}$ c. 25   d. $\dfrac{17}{39}$

10. a. 18   b. $31\dfrac{1}{2}$ c. $4\dfrac{2}{5}$ d. 28

11. a. $1\dfrac{1}{3}$ b. 32   c. $1\dfrac{7}{25}$ d. $\dfrac{1}{18}$

12. a. 14   b. 6   c. $2\dfrac{4}{7}$ d. $\dfrac{3}{8}$

13. a. $\dfrac{1}{6}$ b. $1\dfrac{1}{2}$ c. 9   d. $2\dfrac{1}{2}$

14. a. 18   b. 72   c. 75   d. 72

15. a. >   b. <   c. <

16. a. $1\dfrac{1}{2}$ b. $\dfrac{41}{48}$ c. $1\dfrac{14}{45}$ d. $\dfrac{7}{8}$

17. a. $11\dfrac{1}{48}$ b. $8\dfrac{7}{24}$ c. $25\dfrac{41}{48}$ d. $12\dfrac{5}{12}$

18. a. $\dfrac{5}{36}$ b. $\dfrac{1}{4}$ c. $\dfrac{11}{48}$ d. $\dfrac{7}{40}$

19. a. $5\dfrac{1}{6}$ b. $6\dfrac{1}{4}$ c. $4\dfrac{2}{5}$ d. $\dfrac{1}{3}$

20. a. $4\dfrac{1}{2}$ b. $1\dfrac{7}{10}$ c. $1\dfrac{1}{8}$ d. $5\dfrac{34}{35}$

21. a. $\dfrac{7}{12}$ b. $\dfrac{5}{24}$ c. $\dfrac{5}{16}$

22. a. $\dfrac{1}{6}$ b. $\dfrac{3}{5}$ c. $\dfrac{3}{8}$

23. $49\dfrac{3}{8}$

24. 20 servings

25. $14\dfrac{7}{8}$ pounds

26. $16,000

27. a. 12 yards   b. 40 favors

28. $\dfrac{5}{12}$

29. $\dfrac{7}{24}$

30. a. $P = 25\dfrac{2}{3}$ in.

   $A = 40\dfrac{1}{3}$ sq. in.

   b. $P = 18$ ft.

   $A = 12$ sq. ft.

   c. $P = 11\dfrac{19}{21}$ ft.

   $A = 6$ sq. ft.

   d. $P = 36$ ft.

   $A = 48$ sq. ft.

Answers to Unit 2, Review Form B

1. a. $\{1,2,3,4,6,8,12,24\}$
   b. $\{1,2,3,4,6,8,9,12,18,24,36,72\}$
   c. $\{1,3,17,51\}$

2. a. $2^3 \bullet 3^2$
   b. $2^4 \bullet 3$
   c. 2^6

3. a. 12   b. 16

4. $2\dfrac{3}{5}$ and $\dfrac{13}{5}$

5. a. $6\dfrac{2}{5}$ b. $8\dfrac{1}{2}$ c. $6\dfrac{3}{7}$
   d. $5\dfrac{1}{2}$ e. $6\dfrac{3}{4}$

6. a. $\dfrac{23}{4}$ b. $\dfrac{14}{3}$ c. $\dfrac{33}{5}$
   d. $\dfrac{59}{8}$ e. $\dfrac{17}{5}$

7. a. $\dfrac{2}{3} = \dfrac{18}{27}$ b. $\dfrac{5}{6} = \dfrac{20}{24}$
   c. $\dfrac{5}{9} = \dfrac{25}{45}$ d. $\dfrac{5}{7} = \dfrac{45}{63}$

8. a. $\dfrac{2}{3}$ b. $\dfrac{5}{9}$ c. $\dfrac{2}{5}$
   d. $\dfrac{5}{7}$ e. $\dfrac{3}{50}$

9. a. $\dfrac{3}{16}$ b. $\dfrac{2}{5}$ c. $\dfrac{7}{32}$ d. 25

10. a. $7\dfrac{7}{8}$ b. 12   c. 15   d. $6\dfrac{1}{2}$

11. a. $\dfrac{9}{40}$ b. 48   c. $\dfrac{5}{9}$ d. $\dfrac{1}{9}$

12. a. $2\dfrac{3}{16}$ b. $\dfrac{7}{8}$ c. $1\dfrac{1}{2}$ d. $\dfrac{1}{81}$

13. a. $\dfrac{1}{16}$ b. $1\dfrac{1}{4}$ c. 18   d. $\dfrac{1}{2}$

14. a. 24   b. 60   c. 48   d. 36

15. a. >   b. <   c. <

16. a. $\dfrac{23}{54}$ b. $1\dfrac{5}{21}$ c. $1\dfrac{11}{30}$ d. $\dfrac{47}{90}$

17. a. $6\dfrac{7}{36}$ b. $10\dfrac{1}{21}$ c. $12\dfrac{4}{75}$ d. $9\dfrac{19}{24}$

18. a. $\dfrac{19}{60}$ b. $\dfrac{1}{15}$ c. $\dfrac{1}{4}$ d. $\dfrac{29}{96}$

19. a. $4\dfrac{1}{4}$ b. $3\dfrac{1}{7}$ c. $2\dfrac{2}{3}$ d. $3\dfrac{6}{11}$

20. a. $5\dfrac{1}{2}$ b. $6\dfrac{7}{24}$ c. $\dfrac{4}{5}$ d. $4\dfrac{17}{24}$

21. a. $\dfrac{5}{8}$ b. $\dfrac{11}{27}$ c. $\dfrac{11}{12}$

22. a. $\dfrac{5}{96}$ b. $\dfrac{7}{8}$ c. $\dfrac{1}{3}$

23. $8\frac{1}{24}$ cups

24. 64 bowls

25. $137\frac{7}{8}$ pounds

26. 54 feet

27. a. 6 yards   b. $21

28. $\frac{3}{8}$

29. $\frac{3}{20}$

30. a. $P = 15\frac{1}{2}$ *in.*
$A = 13\frac{1}{8}$ sq. in.

   b. $P = 45$ ft.
$A = 40\frac{1}{2}$ sq. ft.

   c. $P = 10\frac{2}{3}$ *ft.*
$A = 6\frac{1}{9}$ sq. ft.

   d. $P = 25$ ft.
$A = 30$ sq. ft.

Answers to Unit 2,
Multiple Choice Review Form C

1. b

2. d

3. c

4. a

5. b

6. d

7. a

8. d

9. a

10. c

Answers to Unit 2, Review Form D

1. $7\frac{7}{8}$ miles

2. $1\frac{3}{8}$ pounds

3. 174 people

4. $100,800

5. $1\frac{3}{4}$ inches

6. 144 miles

7. $\frac{7}{24}$ left

8. $205

9. a. $24,000   b. $5\frac{1}{4}$ acres

10. a. 19 packages   b. $28\frac{1}{2}$

Math Fundamentals Review

Unit 3

Decimals

1. Round 6.19807 to the nearest

      a. whole number   b. tenth   c. hundredth

2. Round 0 .00719 to the nearest

      a. hundredth   b. thousandth   c. ten-thousandth

Perform the indicated operations:

3. Add: a. $6.84 + 9.2 + 10.089$

            b. $3.25 + 7.895 + 3 \ 1/4$

            c. $8.95 + 15 + 6.85$

4. Subtract: a. $39.807 - 5.61$

            b. $1399.05 - 872.861$

            c. $4 \ ½ - 3.963$

5. Multiply: a. 9.7×0.306

            b. $(8.01)(0.604)$

            c. $89.567 \cdot 10^3$

            d. $0.4019 \cdot 10^6$

            e. $(4.5)^2$

            f. $(0.012)^2$

6. Divide and   a. round to the nearest tenth: $38.65 \div 8.7$

   b. round to the nearest hundredth: $0.01867 \div 0.0031$

Convert the following fractions to decimals and round to the nearest hundredth.

7. $\dfrac{4}{9}$

8. $\dfrac{7}{3}$

9. $3\dfrac{7}{8}$

Convert the following decimals to proper fractions or mixed numbers.

10. 0.65

11. 6.875

12. 0.324

13. Find the perimeter for the following figures:

a.

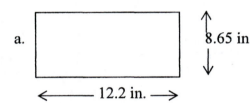

8.65 in.

.

12.2 in.

b.   11.7 in.   9.3 in.

12.6 in.

14. Cindy takes her new car on a weekend trip and drives 76.5 miles on Friday evening, 315.7 miles on Saturday and 274.3 miles on Sunday. How many miles did she drive this weekend?

15. Bob has a scuba diving tank filled with 100 pounds of air pressure. 39.2 pounds of air pressure are used on his first dive. How much air pressure remains in the tank?

16. Your weekly paycheck of $120.70 has $15.79 deducted for taxes and $32.54 deducted for health insurance. How much is your take-home pay?

17. It costs $0.0093 to light an electric bulb for one hour. What is the cost (to the nearest cent) to keep the bulb lit for 250 hours?

18. The aluminum recycling center pays $0.38 per pound for soda cans. What will Carmen receive if he recycles 27.5 pounds of cans?

19. Charlie purchased a yacht for $375,000 and made payments for 21.5 years. What was the payment per year?

20. a. Find the perimeter of a rectangle whose length is 20.6 feet and whose width is 11.7 feet.

b. Find the perimeter of a triangle whose sides are 18.6 inches, 19.9 inches and 22.1 inches.

1. a. Round 8.30971 to the nearest:

     a. hundredth   b. thousandth   c. ten-thousandth

2. Round 0.60502 to the nearest:

     a. whole number   b. tenth   c. thousandth

Perform the indicated operations:

3. Add: a. $9.801 + 4.7 + 30.0865$

                b. $8.02 + 15.7 + 4.387$

                c. $87 \frac{1}{2} + 6.72 + 5$

4. Subtract: a. $3.009 - 2.7$

                b. $918.05 - 487.198$

                c. $4 \frac{3}{4} - 2.375$

5. Multiply: a. 6.3×0.89

                b. $(3.5)(.407)$

                c. $3.924 \cdot 10^2$

                d. $.896 \cdot 10^5$

                e. $(.031)^2$

                f. $(8.6)^2$

6. Divide and: a. round to the nearest tenth: $8.762 \div 5.9$

      b. round to the nearest hundredth: $0.0498 \div 0.0059$

Convert the following fractions to decimals and round to the nearest hundredth:

7. $\dfrac{5}{7}$ 8. $\dfrac{5}{3}$ 9. $2\dfrac{7}{16}$

Convert the following decimals to proper fractions or mixed numbers:

10.   0.85   11.   7.375   12.   0.256

13. Find the perimeter for the following figures:

a.
     9.382 in.

     ← —— 14.79 in. →

b.   6.3 m   5.7 m

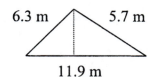

         11.9 m

14. Jesse is a waiter at the Royal Restaurant. His tips for the past four days were $41.50, $36.75, $35 and $29.85. Find the total tips for the four days.

15. Elizabeth received a wage increase from $8.93 per hour to $11.28 per hour. Find the increase in her wages for a 40-hour week.

16. CC Erector Company pays $21.40 per hour for construction ironworkers at the job site during the week and time-and-half over the weekend. What is the pay for 8 hours work on Saturday?

17. Before registration, Chuck has $1,000 in his bank account. If he spent $675 on tuition, he spent $139.75 for books and $39.99 for a tennis racquet, what was the remainder in his account?

18. A condo is purchased at a resort for $250,000. Equal payments are made by the Sprenger family over seventeen years. What was the payment per year? Round to the nearest cent.

19. Kit, a baseball player had 39 hits when he was up at bat 96 times. If a batting average is hits divided by times at bat what is his batting average rounded to the nearest thousandth?

20. a. Find the perimeter of a rectangle whose length is 3.7 meters and whose width is 1.5 meters.

    b. Find the perimeter of a triangle whose sides are 2.6 yards, 4.9 yards and 5.3 yards

1. Round 89.3791 to the nearest thousandth:
    a. 8900   b. 89.379   c. 89.38   d. 89.2

2. Add: 49.3 + 8.601 + 0.089
    a. 57.89   b. 57.989   c. 91.83   d. 57.99

3. Add: $4.032 + 18 + \dfrac{7}{10}$

    a. 22.732   b. 22.802   c. 22.039   d. 29.032

4. Subtract: 60.094 - 3.86
    a. 57.008   b. 56.234   c. 59.708   d. 56.134

5. Subtract: $83.612 - 79\dfrac{5}{8}$

    a. 3.987   b. 3.037   c. 4.037   d. 4.987

6. Multiply: (1.89)(3.2)
    a. 604.8   b. 61.48   c. 6.048   d. 6.148

7. $(5.8)^2$
    a. 25.64   b. 33.54   c. 32.64   d. 33.64

8. Divide and round to the nearest tenth: 89.05 ÷ 0.41
    a. 2.17   b. 21.7   c. 216.2   d. 217.2

9. From a fishing boat, four tuna are caught weighing 52.7, 38.4, 42.9 and 29.6 pounds. What is the total weight of the fish caught?
    a. 153.5 lbs.   b. 163.5 lbs.   c. 163.6 lbs.   d. 153.6 lbs.

10. Cereal is packaged in boxes weighing 24.3 ounces. What is the weight of a case of 48 boxes of cereal?
    a. 116.4 oz.   b. 1165.4 oz.   c. 1167.4 oz.   d. 1166.4 oz.

1. Four pounds of apples cost $2.99, three bananas cost $0.78 and one pineapple costs $1.89. Find the total cost of the fruit.

2. A down payment of $569.49 is placed on a motorcycle costing $7,892.27. Find the amount that remains to be paid.

3. Packaged Oreo cookies are lined in rows of 18 cookies. If each cookie measures .675 inches, find the length of a row of cookies.

4. A $50,000 grant is to be divided evenly among 16 deserving college students for tuition. Find the amount each student will receive.

5. Five days air mileage were noted in a pilot's log book:
    Monday 796.5 miles
    Tuesday 1040.7 miles
    Wednesday 839.6 miles

    Find the total distance flown for the three days.

6. The beginning bank balance is $1,394.60. Find the ending bank balance after deposits of $89.62, $43.90 and $306.98 were made.

7. If bulk mailing costs $0.25 per envelope, how many envelopes can Michelle send for $50?

8. Find the total height of the figure:

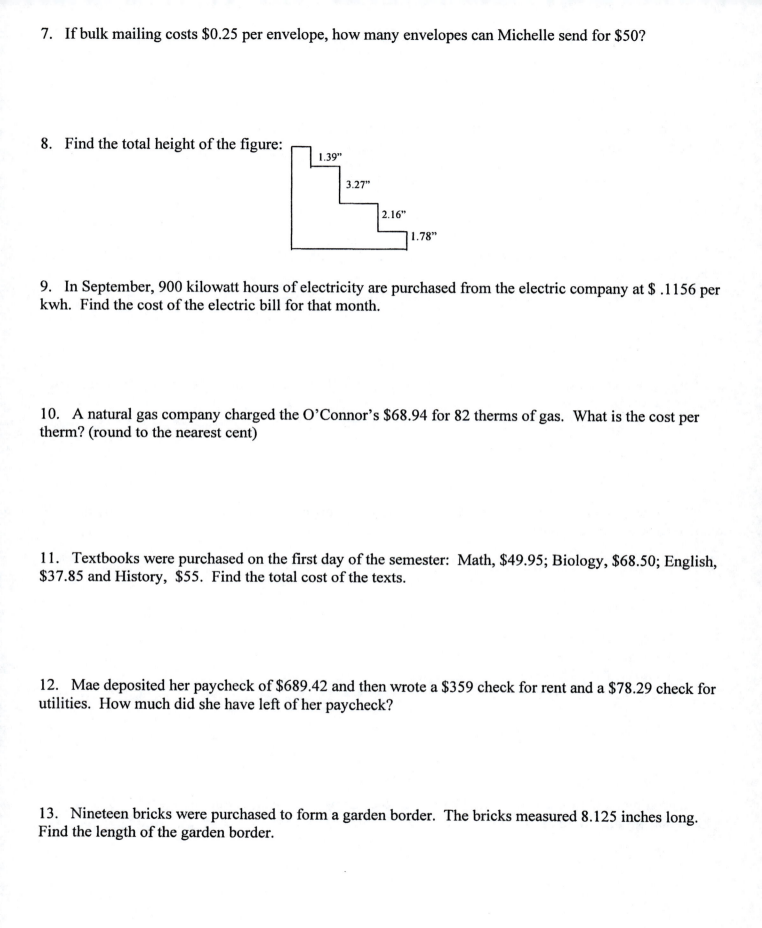

1.39"

3.27"

2.16"

1.78"

9. In September, 900 kilowatt hours of electricity are purchased from the electric company at $ .1156 per kwh. Find the cost of the electric bill for that month.

10. A natural gas company charged the O'Connor's $68.94 for 82 therms of gas. What is the cost per therm? (round to the nearest cent)

11. Textbooks were purchased on the first day of the semester: Math, $49.95; Biology, $68.50; English, $37.85 and History, $55. Find the total cost of the texts.

12. Mae deposited her paycheck of $689.42 and then wrote a $359 check for rent and a $78.29 check for utilities. How much did she have left of her paycheck?

13. Nineteen bricks were purchased to form a garden border. The bricks measured 8.125 inches long. Find the length of the garden border.

14. Four small candles are purchased for $7.98 each and three large candles for $12.49 each. Find the total cost of the seven candles.

15. Find the remaining dimension:

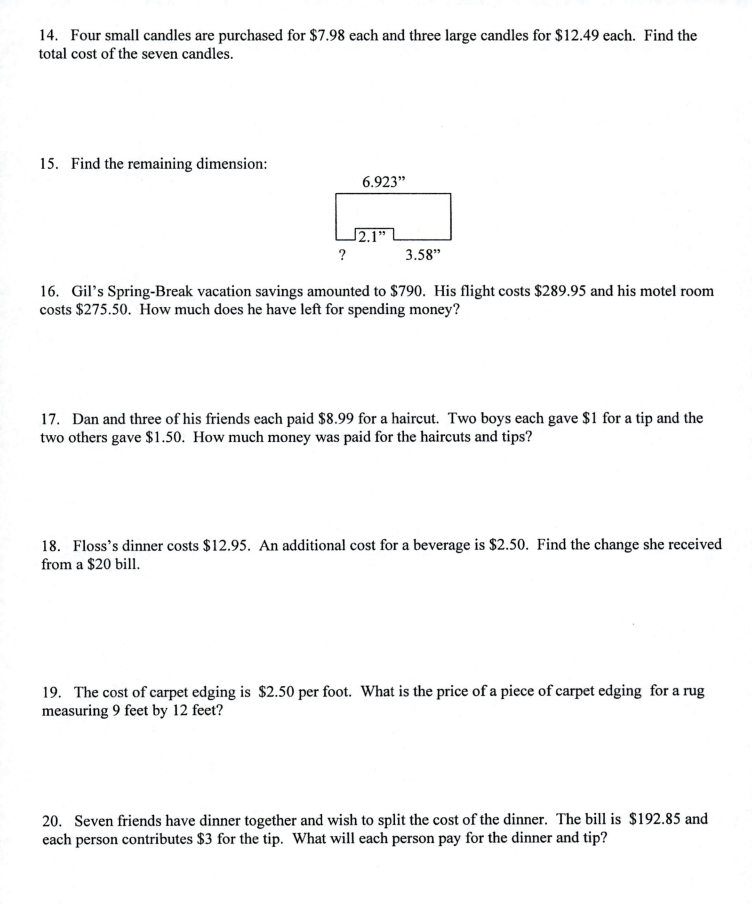

6.923"

2.1"

?   3.58"

16. Gil's Spring-Break vacation savings amounted to $790. His flight costs $289.95 and his motel room costs $275.50. How much does he have left for spending money?

17. Dan and three of his friends each paid $8.99 for a haircut. Two boys each gave $1 for a tip and the two others gave $1.50. How much money was paid for the haircuts and tips?

18. Floss's dinner costs $12.95. An additional cost for a beverage is $2.50. Find the change she received from a $20 bill.

19. The cost of carpet edging is $2.50 per foot. What is the price of a piece of carpet edging for a rug measuring 9 feet by 12 feet?

20. Seven friends have dinner together and wish to split the cost of the dinner. The bill is $192.85 and each person contributes $3 for the tip. What will each person pay for the dinner and tip?

Unit 3
Answers to Review Form A

1. a. 6   b. 6.2   c. 6.20
2. a. 0.01   b. 0.007   c. 0.0072
3. a. 26.129   b.14.395   c. 30.8
4. a. 34.197   b. 526.189   c. 0.537
5. a. 2.9682   b. 4.83804   c. 89,567
    d. 401,900   e. 20.25   f. 0.000144
6. a. 4.4   b. 6.02
7. 0.44
8. 2.33
9. 3.88
10. $\dfrac{13}{20}$

11. $6\dfrac{7}{8}$

12. $\dfrac{81}{250}$

13. a. 41.7 inches   b. 33.6 inches
14. 666.5 miles
15. 60.8 pounds
16. $72.37
17. $2.33
18 $10.45
19. $17,441.86
20. a. 64.6 ft.
    b. 60.6 in.

Unit 3
Answers to Review Form B

1. a. 8.31   b. 8.310   c. 8.3097
2. a. 1   b. .6   c. 0.605
3. a. 44.5875   b. 28.107   c. 99.22
4. a. .309   b. 430.852   c. 2.375
5. a. 5.607   b. 1.426942   c. 392.4
    d. 89,600   e. 0.000961   f. 73.96
6. a. 1.5   b. 8.44
7. 0.71
8. 1.67
9. 2.44
10. $\dfrac{17}{20}$

11. $7\dfrac{3}{8}$

12. $\dfrac{32}{125}$

13. a. 48.344 inches   b. 23.9 m.
14. $143.10
15. $94
16. $256.80
17. $145.26
18. $14,705.88
19. .406
20. a. 10.4 m.
    b. 12.8 yards

Unit 3
Answers to Review Form C

1. b
2. d
3. a
4. b
5. a
6. c
7. d
8. d
9. c
10. d

Unit 3
Answers to Review Form D

1. $5.66
2. $7322.78
3. 12.15 in.
4. $3125
5. 2,676.8 miles
6. $1,835.10
7. 200 env.
8. 8.6 in.
9. $104.04
10. $0.84/therm
11. $211.30.
12. $252.13
13. 154.375 in.
14. $69.39
15. 1.243 in.
16. $244.55
17. $40.96
18. $4.55
19. $105.00
20. $30.55

Math Fundamentals Review

Unit 4

Ratio, Rate, and Proportions

Unit 4
Review Form A

1. Write the following as a ratio is simplest form:
   a. 10 inches to 55 inches

   b. 140 years to 80 years

   c. 32 days to 96 days

   d. 28 ounces to 12 ounces

2. Write the following as a rate in simplest form:
   a. 490 bricks for 21 steps

   b. $180 made in 4 weeks

   c. 1390 miles in 20 days

   d. 250 miles per 15 gallons

3. Write the following as a unit rate:
   a. 15 feet in 4 seconds

   b. 72 cans of paint in 6 days

   c. 540 miles in 12 hours

   d. $89.50 for 10 pounds of steak

4. Determine if the following proportions are true or false:

   a. $\dfrac{3}{4} = \dfrac{5}{6}$

   b. $\dfrac{8}{9} = \dfrac{16}{18}$

   c. $\dfrac{5\,ft.}{\$3} = \dfrac{30\,ft.}{\$18}$

   d. $\dfrac{4lbs.}{15qts.} = \dfrac{12lbs.}{30qts.}$

5. Solve for n and round to the nearest hundredth:

   a. $\dfrac{5}{8} = \dfrac{n}{12}$

   b. $\dfrac{4}{11} = \dfrac{5}{n}$

   c. $\dfrac{8}{n} = \dfrac{12}{16}$

   d. $\dfrac{n}{7} = \dfrac{5}{9}$

HOMEWORK STUDY TIME			
English 40 mins.	Math 75 mins.	Biology 60 mins.	Spanish 35 mins.

Reduce all rates and ratios to lowest terms.

6. Use the table to find the ratio of study time on Math to study time on English.

7. Use the table to find the ratio of study time on Biology to the combined study time of both English and Spanish.

8. Use the table to find the ratio of study time on Math compared to the total time spent in study.

9. 1,550 students attended the concert on Friday evening and 1,300 attended the second performance of the concert on Saturday night. What is the ratio of the number of students attending on Friday to the number attending on Saturday?

10. A tractor is purchased for $130,000 and the trailer for $20,000. What is the ratio of the price of the tractor to the price of the trailer?

11. A car can travel 235 miles on 15 gallons of gas. Express this as a unit rate in simplest form.

12. 125 Amoco stocks were purchased for $1,300. What is the cost per share?

13. 500 computer floppy discs were manufactured for $390. 30 of them were found to be defective. Find the cost per disc for those not defective.

14. It usually takes one shot to drive a golf ball 230 feet from the tee to the green. At this rate, how many shots would it take to drive the golf ball 920 feet?

15. The state tax is 6¢ on every dollar. If a child's wagon costs $18.50, what is the state tax?

16. It takes 3 ounces of putty to install 4 panes of glass. How much putty will be necessary to install 26 panes of glass?

17. 1,000 feet of VHS videotape plays for 1½ hours. How long will it take for Connie to view 300 feet of the videotape?

18. The pilot of USA Airlines has just announced that the plane is travelling at 240 miles per hour. How long will it take for the plane to fly 600 miles?

19. The scale on a map determines that ½ inch represents 300 miles of road. What is the mileage that is represented by 2¼ inches?

20. If 40 pounds of fertilizer will cover 5,000 square feet of lawn, how many pounds of fertilizer will be necessary to properly feed 17,500 square feet of lawn?

21. 500 gallons of water have been pumped into Debbie's pool and she found that the depth of the water measured 1.5 feet. If water is pumped into the pool at the same rate, how many gallons of water will it take to fill the pool to a depth of 6 feet?

22. Repair of a 640 square foot wall of Charlie's barn is necessary. If one panel covers 32 square feet, how many panels are needed to refinish the wall?

23. Taxes on a $50,000 lakeside property are $3,500 per year. What are the taxes on a $20,000 lakeside property?

24. If it takes 15 minutes to run 3 miles, how long will it take to run 10 miles?

25. If 1¼ cups of flour are needed to make three small loaves of bread, how much flour is needed to make 12 small loaves of bread?

1. Write as a ratio is simplest form:

    a. 90¢ to 35¢   b. 14 quarts to 56 quarts

    c. 25 cups to 10 cups   d. 35 minutes to 77 minutes

2. Write as a rate in simplest form:

    a. 75 feet in 10 seconds   b. $3,700 in 15 months

    c. $183 for 12 chairs   d. 85 tomatoes on 20 plants

3. Write as a unit rate:

    a. $165.45 earned in 15 hours   b. 405 miles on 15 gallons of gas

    c. 390 bricks for 3 walls   d. $0.99 for 8 sticks of gum to nearest cent.

4. Determine if the proportion is true or false:

    a. $\dfrac{5}{6} = \dfrac{7}{8}$ b. $\dfrac{2}{15} = \dfrac{4}{30}$ c. $\dfrac{7 lbs.}{12 days} = \dfrac{14 lbs.}{22 days}$ d. $\dfrac{9 yds.}{\$8} = \dfrac{27 yds.}{\$24}$

5. Solve for n and round to the nearest hundredth:

    a. $\dfrac{3}{8} = \dfrac{n}{10}$ b. $\dfrac{5}{9} = \dfrac{12}{n}$ c. $\dfrac{7}{n} = \dfrac{9}{15}$ d. $\dfrac{n}{7} = \dfrac{6}{11}$

COLLEGE REGISTRATION COSTS			
Tuition $1,200	Books $250	Application fee $50	Lab fee $150

Reduce all rates and ratios to lowest terms.

6. Use the table to find the ratio of cost of books to cost of tuition.

7. Use the table to find the ratio of cost of tuition to total cost at registration.

8. Use the table to find the ratio of cost of fees to total cost.

9. Patti purchased a computer for $1,200 and a monitor for $420. What is the ratio of the cost of the monitor to the cost of the computer?

10. There were 1,950 attending a football game at the stadium on Saturday morning and 750 attending the homecoming dinner and dance on Saturday evening. What is the ratio of those attending the evening dinner to those attending the game?

11. Better Paint Store is selling 130 gallons of paint at cost for $2,000. What is the unit rate price for one gallon of paint?

12. An outboard motor on Jim's boat can run for 150 hours on 45 gallons of gas. What is this rate in simplest form?

13. Tom has received his first week's pay check of $389.90 for 35 hours of work in the office. What is his wage per hour?

14. 1,250 ears of corn were harvested at a cost of $76. It was found that 300 ears were harvested too early and could not be sold. What was the price per ear of corn?

15. A gas operated lawn mower requires 4 ounces of oil to every gallon of gas. How many ounces of oil should be mixed with 4½ gallons of gas?

16. In order to form concrete, it is necessary to mix nine wheelbarrows of sand and stone with 2 bags of cement. At this rate, how many bags of cement should be mixed with 30 wheelbarrows of sand and stone? Round to the nearest tenth.

17. If it takes the Public Service Company 3 days to install 2,000 feet of pipe, how long will it take to install 9,000 feet of pipe?

18. Quick Builders promise completion of a 8-room house in 3 months. At this rate, how long should it take them to build a 12-room house?

19. If George can pick 40 baskets of tomatoes in 7 hours, how long will it take him to pick 100 baskets of tomatoes?

20. Connie bought a 15-pack of chewing gum for 89¢. What is the cost of one stick of gum? Round to the nearest cent.

21. Joe's new fishing reel holds 1,900 yards of fishing line. If one spool of line holds 300 yards, how many spools of line should he buy to fill his new reel?

22. Directions on the medication call for a dilution of 2 cc. of the medicine to 15 cc. of distilled water. How much water is to be used for 7 cc. of medicine?

23. The stock exchange reports that Exxon stocks are selling for $67¼. What is the value of 240 stocks?

24. If 600-kilowatt hours of electricity costs $75, what is the cost of electricity for one-kilowatt hour to the nearest cent?

25. A 16 ounce box of Crunchie Cereal is purchased for $2.89. What is the cost of a serving of 2 ounces to the nearest cent?

Unit 4
Multiple Choice Review Form C

1. Write the ratio of 18 days to 27 days in simplest form:
    a. 3 to 2   b. 2 to 3   c. 6 to 9   d. 9 to 6

2. Write the ratio of 5 miles to 150 miles in simplest form:
    a. 1:30   b. 5:150   c. 10:300   d. 150:5

3. Write the rate of 250 words typed in 4 minutes in simplest form:
    a. $\dfrac{250 \text{ words}}{4 \text{ min}}$ b. $\dfrac{250 \text{words}}{2 \text{ min}}$ c. $\dfrac{125 \text{ words}}{2 \text{ min}}$ d. $\dfrac{125 \text{ words}}{4 \text{ min}}$

4. Write $199.75 for 5 pairs of sneakers as a unit rate:
    a. $39.95/pair   b. $39.99/pair   c. $39.85/pair   d. $39.75/pair

5. Which proportion is true?
    a. $\dfrac{5}{7} = \dfrac{10}{15}$ b. $\dfrac{5}{6} = \dfrac{15}{18}$ c. $\dfrac{4}{5} = \dfrac{3}{4}$ d. $\dfrac{6}{7} = \dfrac{8}{9}$

6. Solve: $\dfrac{n}{10} = \dfrac{6}{15}$
    a. n = 5.5   b. n = 5   c. n = 4.5   d. n = 4

7. Solve: $\dfrac{7}{8} = \dfrac{n}{20}$
    a. n = 16.5   b. n = 17   c. n = 17.5   d. n = 18

8. If 3 eggs are used in a recipe for 2 cups of eggnog, how many eggs are needed for 30 cups of egg nog?
    a. 15   b. 20   c. 40   d. 45

9. An 8" by 10" photo is to be enlarged to fit in a frame that is 18" wide. What is the length of the frame for the enlargement?
    a. 22.5"   b. 22"   c. 20.5"   d. 20"

10. If 3 pens cost $0.99, what is the price of 10 pens?
    a. $2.97   b. $3.30   c. $3.50   d. $4.00

Unit 4
Answers to Form A

1. a. 2:11   b. 7:4
   c. 1:3   d. 7:3
2. a. 70 bricks for 3 steps
   b. $45 in 1 week
   c. 139 miles in 2 days
   d. 50 miles per 3 gallons
3. a. 3.75 feet per second
   b. 12 cans per day
   c. 45 miles per hour
   d. $8.95 per pound
4. a. F   b. T   c. T   d. F
5. a. 7.5 b. 13.75 c. 10.67 d. 3.89
6. 15:8
7. 4:5
8. 5:14
9. 31:26
10. 13:2
11. 15.67 miles per gallon
12. $10.40 per share
13. $0.83 per disc
14. 4 shots
15. $1.11
16. 19.5 ounces
17. 0.45 hours or 27 minutes
18. 2 ½ hours
19. 1,350 miles
20. 140 pounds
21. 2,000 gallons
22. 20 panels
23. $1,400
24. 50 minutes
25. 5 cups

Unit 4
Answers to Form B

1. a. 18:7   b. 1:4
   c. 5:2   d. 5:11
2. a. 15 feet in 2 seconds
   b. $740 in 3 months
   c. $61 for 4 chairs
   d. 17 tomatoes on 4 plants
3. a. $11.03 per hour
   b. 27 miles per gallon
   c. 130 bricks for 1 wall
   d. $0.12 per stick of gum
4. a. F   b. T   c. F   d. T
5. a. 3.75 b. 21.6 c. 11.67 d. 3.82
6. 5:24
7. 8:11
8. 4:33
9. 7:20
10. 5:13
11. $15.38 per gal
12. 10 hours : 3 gals
13. $11.14 per hour
14. $0.08 per ear of corn
15. 18 ounces
16. 6.7 bags
17. 13.5 days
18. 4.5 months
19. 17.5 hours
20. $0.06 per stick
21. buy 7 reels, 2/3 reel left over
22. 52.5 cc of water
23. $16,140
24. $0.13
25. $0.36

Unit 4
Answers to Multiple Choice Review Form C

1. b	4. a	7. c	10. b
2. a	5. b	8. d	
3. c	6. d	9. a	

Math Fundamentals Review

Unit 5

Percents

Unit 5
Review Form A

1. Convert $\dfrac{3}{8}$ to a percent.

2. Convert $16\dfrac{2}{3}\%$ to a fraction.

3. Convert 4% to decimal.

4. Convert 1.37 to a percent.

5. Compare $\dfrac{7}{9}$ and 77% using < or >

6. What percent of 200 is 50?

7. What percent of 50 is 200?

8. What is 35% of 250?

9. 45 is 30% of what?

10. 45 is 300% of what?

11. What percent of 63 is 42?

12. What is 0.7% of 140?

13. 105 is what percent of 35?

14. What is $33\dfrac{1}{3}\%$ of 93?

15. 65 is 13% of what?

16. A new drug has an 85% cure rate. If 250 patients are given the drug, how many patients will be cured?

17. A community college has 16,500 students. If 9000 students are women, what percent of the students are women.

18. A survey was distributed and 640 people responded. If this represents 32% of the people who were sent surveys, how many surveys were distributed?

19. 3% of all light bulbs produced at a factory are defective. If a batch of bulbs has 240 defectives, how many bulbs were produced?

20. In 1963 a house was purchased for $15,000. In 1993 that same house was valued at $85,000. What percent of the 1963 price is the 1993 price?

21. A deposit of $160 is made on a furniture purchase. If this represents a 25% down payment, what is the total cost of the furniture?

22. New Jersey has a 6% sales tax. What would the tax be for a $290 television?

23. Noname High School has a 23% dropout rate. If 950 students attend the high school, how many can we expect to graduate?

24. In a given semester 1200 students took the computation portion of the NJCBSPT. If 750 students passed this test, what percent of the students failed?

25. 150 runners begin a marathon. If 18 runners drop out of the race, what percent of the runners finish?

1. Convert $\dfrac{7}{8}$ to a percent.

2. Convert $8\dfrac{1}{3}\%$ to a fraction.

3. Convert 7% to decimal.

4. Convert 2.23 to a percent.

5. Compare $\dfrac{5}{6}$ and 83% using < or >

6. What percent of 150 is 30?

7. What percent of 30 is 150?

8. What is 49% of 350?

9. 24 is 40% of what?

10. 24 is 400% of what?

11. What percent of 195 is 65?

12. What is 0.3% of 120?

13. 108 is what percent of 16?

14. What is $66\dfrac{2}{3}\%$ of 63?

15. 42 is 7% of what?

16. A survey has a 38% return rate. If 1500 people are sent the survey, how many will be returned?

17. 3200 women attend a community college. This represents 64%of the students. How many students attend the college?

18. Noname High School has 1450 students. If 58 students drop out, what percent of the students don't stay in school?

19. New Jersey has a 6% sales tax. If the tax paid for a stereo is $21, how much does the stereo cost including tax?

20. In 1988 a car was purchased for $12,000. In 1994 that same car was valued at $3,600. What percent of the 1988 price is the 1994 price?

21. A deposit of 15% is made on a furniture purchase. If the cost of the furniture is $2500, how much is the deposit?

22. 144 runners finish a race. If this is 80% of the runners that started the race, how many runners started the race?

23. 9000 light bulbs are produced. 270 defective bulbs are found. What percent of the bulbs are acceptable?

24. In a given semester 1400 students took the computation portion of the NJCBSPT and 74% passed. How many students failed the test?

25. A new drug has a 94% cure rate. If 350 patients are given the drug, how many will not be cured?

Unit Five
Multiple Choice Review Form C

1. Convert 35% to a fraction in simplest form.

    a. $\dfrac{35}{100}$ b. $\dfrac{.35}{100}$ c. $\dfrac{7}{20}$ d. $\dfrac{7}{100}$

2. What is 2.5% of 250?

    a. 6.25   b. 62.5   c. 625   d. 6250

3. What percent of 42 is 84?

    a. 20   b. 50%   c. 500%   d. 200%

4. 36% of 720 is what?

    a. 5   b. 20   c. 259.2   d. 2000

5. 28% of what is 126?

    a. 35.28   b. 4.5   c. 45   d. 450

6. What percent of 105 is 3.5?

    a. $3\dfrac{1}{3}\%$ b. $33\dfrac{1}{3}\%$ c. 30%   d. 3%

7. $16\dfrac{2}{3}\%$ of 90 is what?

    a. 150   b. 15   c. $5\dfrac{2}{5}$ d. 54

8. 13% of what is 78?

    a. 10.14   b. 1014   c. 6   d. 600

9. A shirt has been discounted 25%. If the discount is $12, what is the original price?

      a. $3   b. $9   c. $48   d. $15

10. A customer makes a 12% down payment on new furniture. If the payment is $240, how much did the new furniture cost (not including tax)?

      a. $28.80   b. $2000   c. $2880   d. $5000

11. New Jersey charges a 6% sales tax. What would the tax be for a $54 dinner check?

      a. $3.24   b. $32.40   c. $9.00   d. 32¢

12. In a class of 350 students 315 graduate. What percent of the student body failed to graduate?

      a. 90%   b. 10%   c. 111%   d. 35%

13. A basketball player is successful on 65% of her free throws. If she takes 260 shots, how many will she miss?

      a. 169   b. 91   c. 195   d. 65

14. Which is less expensive, a $48 skirt on sale for $\frac{1}{4}$ off or a $70 dress on sale for 50% off?

      a. the skirt at $36   b. the dress at $35   c. the dress at $20   d. the skirt at $12

14. In a certain South Jersey town it rained on 73 days in a year. What percent of the year had rainy days?

      a. 20%   b. 73%   c. 6%   d. 25%

Complete the Chart Below:

	Fraction	Ratio	Decimal	Percent
1	$\frac{3}{4}$			
2		2:5		
3			0.25	
4				5%
5	$\frac{3}{2}$			
6		5:4		
7			1.35	
8				140%
9	$\frac{1}{25}$			
10		1:50		
11			0.07	
12				3%
13	$\frac{1}{200}$			
14		3:25		
15			0.003	
16				0.4%
17	$1\frac{2}{5}$			
18		3:1		
19			0.9	
20				60%

Unit 5
Review Form E

Solve the percent increase or decrease problems below.

1. Samantha weighed 120 lbs. After going on a diet she weighed 108 lbs. What was her percent decrease in weight?

2. Lamar's salary last year was $25,000. This year it is $26,000. What is his percent increase in salary?

3. Janice's childcare center raised its rates from $80 a week to $92 a week. What was the percent increase in price?

4. Calvin used to bench press 150 lbs. Now he can lift 168 pounds. What was his percent increase in weight?

5. Nancy earned $45,000 a year before she received a 5% raise. After the raise, how much did she earn each year?

6. Ron bought a car for $22,000. It has decreased in value by 40%. What is the new value of his car?

Answers to Unit 5, Review Form A

1. 37.5%   2. $\frac{1}{6}$ 3. 0.04   4. 137%

5. $\frac{7}{9} > 77\%$ 6. 25%   7. 400%   8. 87.5

9. 150   10. 15   11. $66\frac{2}{3}\%$ 12. 0.98

13. 300%   14. 31   15. 500   16. 212 or 213

17. 54.5%   18. 2000 surveys   19. 8000 bulbs   20. $566\frac{2}{3}\%$

21. $640   22. $17.40   23. 731 or 732   24. 37.5%

25. 88%

Answers to Unit 5, Review Form B

1. 87.5%   2. $\frac{1}{12}$ 3. 0.07   4. 223%

5. $\frac{5}{6} > 83\%$ 6. 20%   7. 500%   8. 171.5

9. 60   10. 6   11. $33\frac{1}{3}\%$ 12. 0.36

13. 675%   14. 42   15. 600   16. 570 surveys

17. 5000 students   18. 4%   19. $371   20. 30%

21. $375   22. 180 runners   23. 97%   24. 364 students

25. 21 patients

Answers to Unit 5, Multiple Choice Review Form C

1. c   2. a   3. d   4. c   5. d   6. a   7. b   8. d   9. c   10. b   11. a   12. b   13. b   14. b   15. a

Answers to Unit 5, Review Form E

1. 10%   2. 4%   3. 15%   4. 12%   5. $47,250   6. $13,200

	Fraction	Ratio	Decimal	Percent
1	$\frac{3}{4}$	3:4	0.75	75%
2	$\frac{2}{5}$	2:5	0.4	40%
3	$\frac{1}{4}$	1:4	0.25	25%
4	$\frac{1}{20}$	1:20	0.05	5%
5	$\frac{3}{2}$	3:2	1.5	150%
6	$1\frac{1}{4}$ or $\frac{5}{4}$	5:4	1.25	125%
7	$1\frac{7}{20}$ or $\frac{27}{20}$	27:20	1.35	135%
8	$1\frac{2}{5}$ or $\frac{7}{5}$	7:5	1.4	140%
9	$\frac{1}{25}$	1:25	0.04	4%
10	$\frac{1}{50}$	1:50	0.02	2%
11	$\frac{7}{100}$	7:100	0.07	7%
12	$\frac{3}{100}$	3:100	0.03	3%
13	$\frac{1}{200}$	1:200	0.005	0.5%
14	$\frac{3}{25}$	3:25	0.12	12%
15	$\frac{3}{1000}$	3:1000	0.003	0.3%
16	$\frac{1}{250}$	1:250	0.004	0.4%
17	$1\frac{4}{5}$	9:5	1.8	180%
18	3	3:1	3	300%
19	$\frac{9}{10}$	9:10	0.9	90%
20	$\frac{3}{5}$	3:5	0.6	60%

Math Fundamentals Review

Unit 6

Statistics

Unit 6

Review Form A

The pictograph in Figure 1 shows the number of sundaes sold at an ice cream parlor on Friday, Saturday, and Sunday. Each picture represents four sundaes.

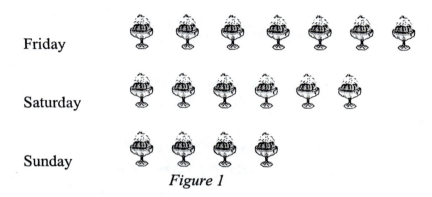

Friday

Saturday

Sunday

Figure 1

1. Find the total number of sundaes sold over the three days.

2. Find the ratio of the number of sundaes sold on Sunday to the number of sundaes sold on Saturday.

3a. Find the percent of the total number of sundaes that were sold on Saturday. (Round answer to nearest percent.)

3b. Find the percent decrease of sundaes sold from Saturday to Sunday.

The circle graph in Figure 2 shows the percent of income budgeted in a household for a year. If the family has a yearly income of $40,000, find the following:

4. How much money is allocated for food ?

5. How much money is allocated for rent ?

6. Find the ratio of the amount allowed for entertainment to the amount of funds allotted for education.

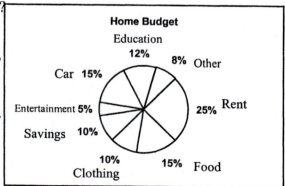

Figure 2

7. How much more will be spent on food than on clothes ?

64

The bar graph in Figure 3 shows the total 1993 sales of houses in Highland County.

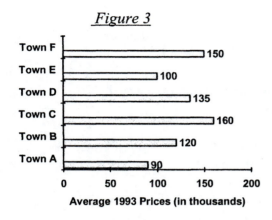

Figure 3

Average 1993 Prices (in thousands)

8. Which town in Highland County had the highest average selling price ?

9. What was the 1993 average selling price for a home in Town D ?

10a. Find the ratio of the average selling price of a house in Town A to the average selling price of a house in Town B.

10b. Find the percent increase in sales from Town B to Town F.

The double-bar graph in Figure 4 shows the quarterly profits for a company for the years 1992 and 1993.

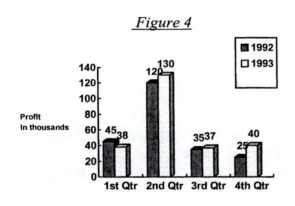

Figure 4

11. Find the amount of profit in the third quarter of 1992.

12. In what quarter of 1993 did the company have the most profit ?

13a. Find the difference in profit between 1992 and 1993 in the fourth quarter.

13b. Find the percent increase in profits from 1992 to 1993 in the 4th quarter.

The double broken-line graph in Figure 5 shows the daily high and low temperatures in degrees Fahrenheit for a week.

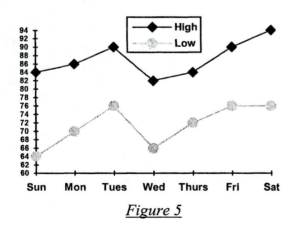

Figure 5

14. Find the high temperature for Tuesday.

15. Find the difference between the low temperatures on Sunday and Tuesday.

16. What is the percent decrease in low temperatures from Friday to Saturday?

The bar graph in Figure 6 shows the number of students earning A, B, C, D and F grades in a math test.

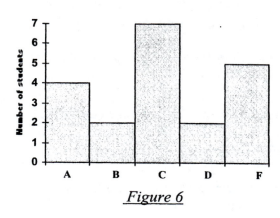

Figure 6

17. How many students achieved an "A" in the test ?

18. How many students passed the test ?

19. Find the percent of students who failed the test.

20. Find the ratio of the number of students who passed the test to the total number of students in the class.

21. In a gymnastic competition Jon scored 8.7, 8.9, 9.2, 9.0, and 9.2 respectively from five different judges.
    a. Find Jon's mean score.
    b. Find Jon's median score.
    c. Find the mode.

22. In one week a used car dealership sold eight cars at the following prices: $15,000, $9,500, $5,000, $8,000, $10,500, $11,000, $13,000 and $9,000.
    a. Find the median price of a car sold for the week. *(Round answer to nearest dollar)*
    b. Find the mean selling price of a car for the week. *(Round answer to nearest dollar)*

Unit 6

Review Form B

The pictograph in Figure 1 shows the number of boxes of popcorn sold at the movies on Friday, Saturday, and Sunday. Each picture represents 20 boxes.

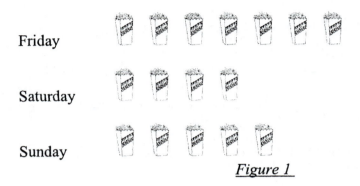

Friday

Saturday

Sunday

Figure 1

1. Find the total number of boxes of popcorn sold Saturday and Sunday.

2. Find the ratio of the number of boxes sold on Friday to the number of boxes sold on Saturday.

3a. Find the percent of the total number of boxes sold on Saturday.

3b. Find the percent decrease in number of boxes sold from Sunday to Saturday.

The circle graph in Figure 2 shows the percent of car expenses for a year. If the total car expense for the year is $7000, find the following:

4. How much money is allocated for insurance ?

5. How much money is allocated for gas ?

6. Find the ratio of the amount allowed for gas to the amount allowed for maintenance.

7. How much more money will be spent on insurance than maintenance ?

Insurance
Car Payment
Gas
Maintenance

Gas 6%
Maintenance 12%
Insurance 21%
Car Payment 61%

Figure 2

The bar graph in Figure 3 shows April car sales in local dealerships.

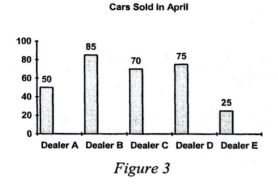

Cars Sold in April

Figure 3

8. Which dealer had the highest sales for the month ?

9. How many cars were sold by Dealer D in April ?

10a. Find the ratio of the number of cars sold by Dealer E to the number of cars sold by Dealer D.

10b. Find the percent decrease in sales from Dealer A to Dealer E.

The double-bar graph in Figure 4 shows the number of VCRs sold by a wholesale club for the last four months of 2002 and 2003.

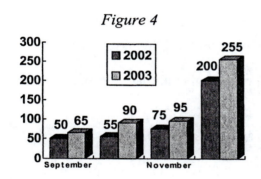

Figure 4

11. Find the number of VCRs sold in December, 2003.

12. In what month in 2002 were the most VCRs sold ?

13a. Find the difference in sales between October and November in 2002.

13b. Find the percent increase in sales in September.

The double broken-line graph in Figure 5 shows the quarterly sales for a company for the years 1992 and 1993.

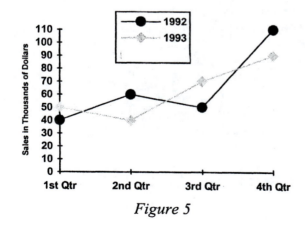

Figure 5

14. Find the sales for the third quarter of 1993.

15. In 1992, which quarter had the lowest sales ?

16a. Find the difference between the company's second quarter sales for 1992 and 1993.

16b. Find the percent decrease is sales in the 2nd quarter?

The bar graph in Figure 6 shows the number of students enrolled in a university from 2000 to 2003.

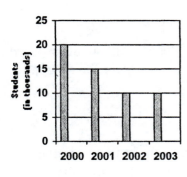

Figure 6

17. How many students were enrolled in 2001?

18. Find the ratio of the number of students enrolled in 2003 to the number of students enrolled in 2000.

19. Find the percent decrease in the number of students enrolled in 2000 to the number of students enrolled in 2003.

20. In which year was the number of students enrolled the greatest?

21. Dan scored 85, 90, 70, 80, 95, and 70 on six algebra tests.
   a. Find Dan's mean score. *(Round to the nearest whole number)*
   b. Find Dan's median score.
   c. Find the mode.

22. Sharon purchased books at the college book store last week for $45.00, $50.00 $35.00, $60.00, and $70.00.
   a. Find the median price of the books that Sharon purchased.
   b. Find the mean purchase price of the books that Sharon purchased last week.

Unit 6

Review Form C

The circle graph in Figure 1 shows the annual expenses for a student at college.

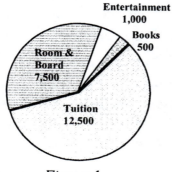

Figure 1

1. Find the ratio of the amount spent for room & board to the amount spent for tuition.

   a. $\frac{5}{3}$ b. $\frac{3}{5}$ c. $\frac{1}{15}$ d. $\frac{1}{25}$

2. What is the ratio of the amount spent on books to the amount spent on tuition and room and board ?

   a. $\frac{1}{5}$ b. $\frac{1}{2}$ c. $\frac{1}{15}$ d. $\frac{1}{40}$

The double-bar graph in Figure 2 shows the number of computers sold by a computer dealer for the last four months of 2002 and 2003.

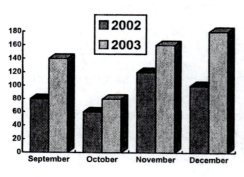

Figure 2

3. Find the number of computers sold in October 2003.

   a. 80   b. 60   c. 120   d. 160

4. In what month in 2002 were the least computers sold ?

   a. Sept.   b. Oct.   c. Nov.   d. Dec.

5. Find the percent increase in sales from September 2002 to September 2003 ?

   a. 57%   b. 43%   c. 75%   d. 25%

The double broken-line graph in Figure 3 shows the quarterly sales for a company for the years 1992 and 1993.

Figure 3

6. In 1993, which quarter had the highest sales ?

   a. 1st   b. 2nd   c. 3rd   d. 4th

7. Find the percent increase in sales in 1992 from the 3rd quarter to the 4th quarter.

   a. 40%   b. 50%   c. 100%   d. 86%

8. Find the difference between the company's second quarter sales for 1992 and 1993.

   a. $20,000   b. $30,000   c. $40,000   d. $50,000

The graph in Figure 4 shows the high temperatures in Camden, New Jersey for a week in July.

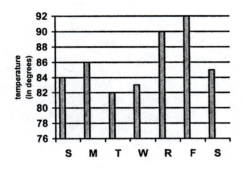

9. Find the mean high temperature for the week.
a. 82   b. 86   c. 85   d. 92

10. Find the median high temperature for the week.
a. 85   b. 86   c. 92   d. 87

Answers to Unit 6, Review Form A

1. 68
2. $\frac{2}{3}$
3a. 35%, 3b. $33\frac{1}{3}$%
4. $6,000
5. $10,000
6. $\frac{5}{12}$
7. $2,000
8. Town C
9. $135,000
10a. $\frac{3}{4}$, 10b. 25%
11. $35,000
12. 2nd quarter
13a. $15,000, 13b. 60%
14. 90°
15. 12°
16. 0 %
17. 4
18. 15
19. 25%
20. $\frac{3}{4}$
21a. 9.0   b. 9.0   c. 9.2
22a. $10,000   b. $10,125

Answers to Unit 6, Review Form B

1. 180
2. $\frac{7}{4}$
3a. 25%, 3b. 20%
4. $1,470
5. $420
6. $\frac{1}{2}$
7. $630
8. Dealer B
9. 75
10a. $\frac{1}{3}$, 10b. 50%
11. 255
12. December
13a. 20   b. 30%
14. $70,000
15. First quarter
16a $20,000 16b. 33.3%
17. 15,000
18. $\frac{1}{2}$
19. 50%
20. 2000
21a. 82   b. 82.5   c. 70
22a. $50.00   b. $52.00

Answers to Unit 6, Review Form C

1. b
2. d
3. a
4. b
5. c
6. d
7. c
8. b
9. b
10. a

Math Fundamentals Review

Unit 7

U. S. Customary Units of Measure

Provide the indicated equivalent

1. 5 ft = _____ in

2. 36 ft = _____ yd

3. 5 yd = _____ ft

4. 48 in = _____ ft

5. 4 yd = _____ in

6. 72 in = _____ yd

7. 96 oz = _____ lb

8. 6000 lb = _____ tons

9. 5 tons = _____ lb

10. 8 lb = _____ oz

11. 5 gal = _____ qt

12. 48 pt = _____ qt

13. 14 pt = _____ c

14. 20 c = _____ fl oz

15. 18 qt = _____ g

16. 18 qt = _____ pt

17. 14 c = _____ pt

18. 3 gal = _____ pt

19. 4 qt = _____ c

20. 64 fl oz = _____ qt

Provide the indicated equivalent

1. 7 ft = _____ in

2. 42 ft = _____ yd

3. 9 yd = _____ ft

4. 36 in = _____ ft

5. 5 yd = _____ in

6. 108 in = _____ yd

7. 80 oz = _____ lb

8. 8000 lb = _____ tons

9. 3 tons = _____ lb

10. 5 lb = _____ oz

11. 9 gal = _____ qt

12. 40 pt = _____ qt

13. 22 pt = _____ c

14. 15 c = _____ fl oz

15. 10 qt = _____ g

16. 20 qt = _____ pt

17. 18 c = _____ pt

18. 5 gal = _____ pt

19. 3 qt = _____ c

20. 96 fl oz = _____ qt

1. 16 qt =   a. 64 gal   b. 32 gal   c. 8 gal   d. 4 gal

2. 100 yd =   a. 300 ft   b. 1200 ft   c. $33\frac{1}{3}$ ft   d. $8\frac{1}{3}$ ft

3. 96 oz =   a. 6 lb   b. 8 lb   c. 9.6 lb   d. 1536 lb

4. 48 pt =   a. 96 qt   b. 24 qt   c. 12 qt   d. 6 qt

5. 120 in =   a. 60 ft   b. 40 ft   c. 12 ft   d. 10 ft

6. 8000 lbs =   a. 8 tons   b. 4 tons   c. 2 tons   d. 1 ton

7. Which is the largest measure:

    a. 4 qt   b. 2 gal   c. 64 fl oz   d. 10 pt

8. Which is the smallest measure:

    a. 14 yd   b. 40 ft   c. 400 in

9. Which of the following measures is not equivalent to the others:

    a. 64 fl oz   b. 8 c   c. 4 pt   d. 1 qt

10. Which of the symbols below should be used to fill in the blank: 480 oz _____ 32 lb

    a. >   b. <   c. =

Answers to Unit 7, Review Form A

1. 60	2. 12	3. 15	4. 4	5. 144	6. 2
7. 6	8. 3	9. 10000	10. 128	11. 20	12. 24
13. 28	14. 160	15. 4.5	16. 36	17. 7	18. 24
19. 16	20. 2				

Answers to Unit 7, Review Form B

1. 84	2. 14	3. 27	4. 3	5. 180	6. 3
7. 5	8. 4	9. 6000	10. 80	11. 36	12. 20
13. 44	14. 120	15. 2.5	16. 40	17. 9	18. 40
19. 12	20. 3				

Answers to Unit 7, Review Form C

1. d   2. a   3. a   4. b   5. d   6. b   7. b   8. c   9. d   10. b

Math Fundamentals Review

Unit 8

The Metric System of Measurement

Choose the most reasonable metric measure

1. The width of a classroom

    a. 8.5 km   b. 8.5 m   c. 8.5 cm   d. 8.5 mm

2. The temperature of a cup of hot tea

    a. $0°$ C   b. $10°$ c. $50°$ d. $150°$

3. The weight of a professional football player

    a. 250 kg   b. 115 kg   c. 50 kg   d. 10 kg

4. The amount of gasoline used to drive 25 miles

    a. 4 L   b. 4 mL   c. 4 cL   d. 4 kL

5. The weight of a hamburger

    a. 100 mg   b. 100 cg   c. 100 g   d. 100 kg

For problems 6 through 10, circle the smaller amount

6. $32°$ F $10°$ C

7.   200 lb   100 kg

8.   25 mm   3 cm

9.   900 mL   1 qt

10.   5 ft   100 cm

Complete each statement (round to the nearest thousandth where necessary)

11. 10 km = _____ m

12. 22 m = _____ km

13. 500 cm = _____ m

14. 50 L = _____ mL

15. 45 cm^3 = _____ mL

16. 500 mg = _____ g

17. 23 g = _____ mg

18. 400 m = _____ cm

19. 3000mm = _____ cm

20. 500 cm^3 = _____ L

21. 23 cm = _____ in

22. 25 in = _____ cm

23. 16 fl oz = _____ mL

24. 45 mi = _____ km

25. 50° F = _____ C

26. 8 L = _____ qt

27. 400 kg = _____ lb

28. 25° C = _____ F

29. 8 fl oz = _____ cm^3

30. 24 g = _____ oz

Form B

Choose the most reasonable metric measure

1. The width of a sheet of notebook paper

    a. 22 km   b. 22 m   c. 22 cm   d. 22 mm

2. The temperature of a milkshake

    a. 0° C   b. 5° C   c. 30° C   d. 50° C

3. The weight of an adult cat

    a. 120 kg   b. 24 kg   c. 12 kg   d. 6 kg

4. The amount of soda in a can

    a. 360 mL   b. 360 cL   c. 360 L   d. 360 kL

5. The weight of a newborn baby

    a. 4000 mg   b. 4000 g   c. 4000 kg   d. 40 kg

For Problems 6 – 10 circle the larger amount

6.   200° F   100° C

7.   5 yd   5 m

8.   500 mg   1 g

9.   4 L   1 gal

10.   12 in   30 cm

Complete each statement (round to the nearest thousandth where necessary)

11. 15 km = _____ m

12. 35 m = _____ km

13. 200 cm = _____ m

14. 40 L = _____ mL

15. 25 cm^3 = _____ mL

16. 200 mg = _____ g

17. 43 g = _____ mg

18. 800 m = _____ cm

19. 2000mm = _____ cm

20. 300 cm^3 = _____ L

21. 18 cm = _____ in

22. 45 in = _____ cm

23. 12 fl oz = _____ mL

24. 75 mi = _____ km

25. 86° F = _____ C

26. 5 L = _____ qt

27. 800 kg = _____ lb

28. 15° C = _____ F

29. 6 fl oz = _____ cm^3

30. 64 g = _____ oz

Choose the most reasonable metric measure

1. The speed a car drives on a turnpike

    a. 30 km/h   b. 60 km/h   c. 100 km/h   d. 200 km/h

2. The dosage of allergy medicine prescribed

    a. 25 mg   b. 25 cg   c. 25 g   d. 25 kg

Choose the correct equivalent

3. 70 mg =

    a. 0.007 g   b. 0.07 g   c. 0.7 g   d. 7g

4. 6500 m =

    a. 6.5 km   b. 65 km   c. 650 km   d. 65,000 km

5. 5 mL =

    a. 5 cm^3 b. 15 cm^3 c. 125 cm^3 d. 5000 cm^3

6. 30 L =

    a. 300 mL   b. 3000 mL   c. 30,000 mL   d. 300,000 mL

7. 35°C =

    a. 1.7°F   b. 31°F   c. 70°F   d. 95°F

8. 350 mi =

    a. 560 km   b. 217 km   c. 565 km   d. 219 km

9. 15 gal =

    a. 14.3 L   b. 15.9 L   c. 57 L   d. 63.6 L

10. 500 g =

    a. 1.1 lb   b. 0.225 lb   c. 14,000 lb   d. 225 lb

Answers to Unit 8, Review Form A

1. b	2. c	3. b	4. a	5. c
6. 32 °F	7. 200 lb	8. 2.5 mm	9. 900 mL	10. 100 cm
11. 10 000	12. 0.022	13. 5	14. 50 000	15. 45
16. 0.5	17. 23 000	18. 40 000	19. 300	20. 0.5
21. 9.062	22. 63.5	23. 480	24. 72	25. 10
26. 8.48	27. 880	28. 77	29. 240	30. 0.857

Answers to Unit 8, Review Form B

1. c	2. b	3. d	4. a	5. b
6. 100 °C	7. 5m	8. 1g	9. 4L	10. 12in
11. 15 000	12. 0.035	13. 2	14. 40 000	15. 25
16. 0.2	17. 43 000	18. 80 000	19. 200	20. 0.3
21. 7.092	22. 114.3	23. 360	24. 120	25. 30
26. 5.3	27. 1760	28. 59	29. 180	30. 2.286

Answers to Unit 8, Review Form C

1. c	2. a	3. b	4. a	5. a
6. c	7. d	8. a	9. c	10. a

Math Fundamentals Review

Unit 9

Geometry

Unit 9

Review Form A

1. Find the perimeter of a rectangle with a width of 4.3 ft. and a length of 8.2 ft.

2. Find the circumference of a circle with a diameter of 16 in.

3. Find the area of a rectangle with a width of .35 in. and a length of 2.75 in.

4. Find the perimeter of a triangle whose sides measure $1\frac{1}{4}$", $1\frac{1}{8}$" and $1\frac{1}{4}$".

5. Find the area of a triangle whose base is 10" and whose height is 16".

6. What is the area of a circle whose radius is 7 in. ?

7. Find the area of a concrete driveway 18 ft. long by 12 ft. wide.

8. How much would it cost to install fencing around a garden 5 ft. long by 3 ft. wide if fencing costs $3.50 per foot ?

9. How much would it cost to carpet a room 17 ft. long and 15 ft. wide if the carpet costs $3.25 a square foot ?

10. A jogger runs around a circular path with a diameter of 900 yards. If he runs around the path twice, how far has he run?

Unit 9

Review Form B

1. Find the area of a rectangle with a width of 5 ft. and a length of 9 ft.

2. Find the perimeter of a rectangle with a length of 35in. and a width of 17in.

3. Find the circumference of a circle with a radius of 100 in.

4. Find the perimeter of a square whose side measures 8 inches.

5. Find the area of a triangle whose base is 9" and whose height is 6".

6. Find the area of a circle whose diameter is 16".

7. How much would it cost to install ceramic tile in a kitchen 10 ft. long and 8 ft. wide if the contractor asked $17 a square foot to do the job including the labor and the cost of the tile?

8. How much would it cost to put a fence around a circular area having a radius of 6 ft. if fencing costs $3.25 per foot ?

9. How much weather stripping is needed to put around a door 8 ft. high and 3 ft. wide ?

10. A circular glass top coffee table has a radius of 20 in. Find the area of the table top.

Unit 9

Review Form C

1. Find the area of a circle with a radius of 4 inches.

    a. 12.56 in^2 c. 25.12 in^2

    b. 50.24 in^2 d. 200.96 in^2

2. Find the circumference of a circle whose radius is 5 inches .

    a. 78.50 in   c. 15.7 in

    b. 3.14 in   d. 31.40 in

Find the area of the following figures.

3.

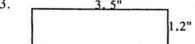

3. 5"

1.2"

    a. 4.7 in^2 c. 4.2 in^2

    b. 9.4 in^2 d. 2.1 in^2

4.

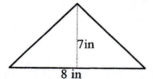

7in

8 in

    a. 56 in^2 c. 15in^2

    b. 28 in^2 d. 57 in^2

Find the circumference of the following figure.

5.

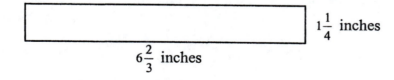

$1\frac{1}{4}$ inches

$6\frac{2}{3}$ inches

    a. $8\frac{1}{3}$ inches   c. $7\frac{11}{12}$ inches

    b. $15\frac{5}{6}$ inches   d. $15\frac{1}{2}$ inches

Find the perimeter of the following figure.

6.

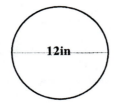

12in

   a. 113.04 in   c. 37.68 in

   b. 18.84 in   d. 452.16 in

7. A plate glass window for a store measures 6 ft by 6 ft. If glass costs $12 per square foot, how much will it cost to replace the window?

   a. $288   c. $432

   b. $216   d. $244

8. If fencing costs $3.95 per foot, how much would it cost to fence a rectangular area 85 ft. by 25 ft.?

   a. $869   c. $839.38

   b. $2125   d. $434.50

9. How much would it cost to carpet a room 15 ft. long and 12 ft. wide if the carpet costs $3.50 a square foot?

   a. $5670   c. $1701

   b. $630   d. $850.50

10. If fencing costs $3.75 per foot, how much would it cost to fence a rectangular area 80 ft. by 20 ft.?

   a. $6000   c. $1600

   b. $750   d. $200

**Answers to Unit 9
Review Form A**

1. 25 ft
2. 50.24 in
3. .9625 in^2
4. $3\frac{5}{8}$
5. 80 in^2
6. 153.86 in^2
7. 216 ft^2
8. $56
9. $828.75
10. 5652 yds.

**Answers to Unit 9
Review Form B**

1. 45 ft^2
2. 104 in
3. 628 in
4. 32 in
5. 27 in^2
6. 200.96 in^2
7. $1360
8. $122.46
9. 22 ft
10. 1256 in^2

**Answers to Unit 9
Review Form C**

1. b
2. d
3. c
4. b
5. b
6. c
7. c
8. a
9. b
10. b

Math Fundamentals Review

Comprehensive Review

Comprehensive Review

Multiple Choice Questions

1. Write thirty-two thousand twenty-one in standard form.
   - a. 3221
   - b. 32,210
   - c. 32,021
   - d. 32,000,021

2. Simplify: $16 - 4(5 - 2) \div 2$
   - a. 1
   - b. 18
   - c. 10
   - d. 2

3. Grandpop's will required that his estate should be divided equally among his twelve grandchildren. If each grandchild received $33,569, how much was Grandpop's estate worth?
   - a. $100,707
   - b. $402,828
   - c. $402,818
   - d. $2,797

4. Shannon went on a shopping spree. He bought a $24 shirt, an $8 tie, and a pair of $60 shoes. How much change did he get from a $100 bill?
   - a. $92
   - b. $16
   - c. $84
   - d. $8

5. John has 7, 296 heads of lettuce ready for the market. If he packs twenty-four heads per box, how many boxes of lettuce can he ship?
   - a. 175,104
   - b. 34
   - c. 3,004
   - d. 304

6. Add: $5\dfrac{3}{8} + 7\dfrac{5}{6}$
   - a. $13\dfrac{5}{24}$
   - b. $35\dfrac{8}{14}$
   - c. $12\dfrac{5}{24}$
   - d. $12\dfrac{4}{7}$

7. Subtract: $15\dfrac{3}{10} - 5\dfrac{5}{6}$
   - a. $10\dfrac{1}{2}$
   - b. $10\dfrac{7}{15}$
   - c. $9\dfrac{7}{15}$
   - d. $10\dfrac{8}{15}$

8. Multiply: $5\dfrac{1}{7} \cdot 7\dfrac{5}{6}$
   - a. $35\dfrac{5}{42}$
   - b. $35\dfrac{1}{7}$
   - c. $12\dfrac{6}{13}$
   - d. $40\dfrac{2}{7}$

9. Divide: $4\dfrac{3}{8} \div 2\dfrac{1}{3}$

   a. $2\dfrac{1}{8}$ b. $10\dfrac{5}{24}$ c. $4\dfrac{3}{8}$ d. $1\dfrac{7}{8}$

10. Simplify: $\dfrac{5}{8} - \left(\dfrac{1}{2}\right)^2 \bullet \dfrac{2}{3}$

    a. $\dfrac{11}{24}$ b. $\dfrac{25}{24}$ c. $\dfrac{1}{4}$ d. $\dfrac{7}{24}$

11. Multiply and round to the nearest tenth: $(4.09)^2$

    a. 16.1   b. 16.81   c. 16.7   d. 16.72

12. Divide and round to the nearest hundredth: $0.3384 \div 0.092$

    a. 3.68   b. 3.678   c. 3.69   d. 3.70

13. Convert 10.375 to a mixed number.

    a. $10\dfrac{37}{100}$ b. $10\dfrac{3}{10}$ c. $10\dfrac{3}{8}$ d. $\dfrac{10}{375}$

14. It costs $339.95 for a round trip airline ticket to Florida. Find the total cost for a family of five to fly to Florida.

    a. $1699.25   b. $1689.25   c. $1969.75   d. $1699.75

15. A mountain resort home owner has to pay taxes of $586.75 every three months. What taxes are paid on this home for one year?

    a. $1173.50   b. $2347.00   c. $3520.50   d. $7041.00

16. Solve for n and round to the nearest hundredth: $\dfrac{6}{7} = \dfrac{17}{n}$

    a. 19.73   b. 19.83   c. 19.88   d. 19.93

17. If it takes 47 minutes to walk 7 miles, how long will it take to walk 9 miles? Round to the nearest minute.

    a. 57   b. 59   c. 60   d. 61

18. 30 shares of AT&T stock were purchased for $8,250. What is the cost of ten shares?

    a. $2750.00   b. $270.50   c. 27.50   d. 275.00

19. Computer paper is sold for $50.00 per box of 5,000 sheets. What is the unit rate price for one sheet of paper, rounded to the nearest cent?

    a. $ .01   b. $ .11   c. $ .02   d. $ .10

20. An 8 ½ " wide by 11" long piece of paper is to be enlarged to poster size. If the width is enlarged to be 34", what is the new measurement of the length?

    a. 26.2"   b. 26.3"   c. 42"   d. 44"

21. Convert $\frac{5}{8}$ to a percent.

    a. 5.8 %   b. 6.25 %   c. 62.5 %   d. 625 %

22. What percent of 33 is 66?

    a. 20 %   b. 50 %   c. 200 %   d. 500 %

23. 72 % of what is 234?

    a. 325   b. 162   c. 225   d. 306

24. A stereo costs $280 (not including tax). $19.60 must be paid for sales tax. What percent of the cost is the tax?

    a. 6 %   b. 7 %   c. 14 %   d. 19.6 %

25. 240 runners begin a race. Only 75 % of the runners finish. How many runners do not finish the race?

    a. 180   b. 60   c. 165   d. 75

26. A home is selling for $87,000. The lender requires a 12 % down payment. How much is the required down payment?

    a. $7250   b. $8700   c. $10,440   d. $12,000

27. A student needs 60% to pass a test containing 40 questions. How many questions does the student need to get right?

    a. 24   b. 16   c. 7   d. 30

28. A company hired 24 new employees this year. If this was a 12% increase, how many employees did the company have before the increase?

    a. 3   b. 200   c. 224   d. 100

29. A sales clerk earned $162.50 for working 25 hours. What is the hourly wage?

    a. $6.50   b. $5.05   c. $112.50   d. $180

30. A secretary makes double time when working overtime. If her normal salary is $7.50 per hour and she works 12 hours of overtime, how much extra will she make?

    a. $90   b. $62.50   c. $112.50   d. $180

31. Simplify: $9 + 4.1 - 7.21 + 0.003$

    a. 20.313   b. 5.893   c. 23.92   d. 8.89

32. Subtract: $5.03 - 2.927$

    a. 2.103   b. 2.404   c. 2.113   d. 3.887

33. Simplify: $0.845 + \dfrac{3}{8}$

    a. 0.8453   b. 0.1220   c. 84.53   d. 1.22

34. Simplify: $\dfrac{12}{\frac{3}{4}}$

    a. 1   b. 9   c. 16   d. 2

35. Simplify: $(4.6)^2$

    a. 21.16   b. 9.2   c. 4.8   d. 16.36

36. Multiply: (2.7)(70.04)

    a. 189.808   b. 189.108   c. 72.74   d. 1891.08

37. What is 64.05 divided by 6.1 ?

    a. 1.05   b. 105   c. 10.5   d. 0.105

38. What is 65 divided by 0.5?

    a. 13   b. 1.3   c. 1300   d. 130

39. Simplify: $0.83 + \dfrac{7}{10}$

    a. 0.90   b. 1.53   c. 0.153   d. 9.0

40. Add: $4\dfrac{1}{4} + \dfrac{7}{12}$

    a. $4\dfrac{5}{6}$ b. $4\dfrac{1}{2}$ c. $\dfrac{5}{6}$ d. $4\dfrac{2}{3}$

41. Subtract: $\dfrac{7}{8} - \dfrac{1}{3}$

    a. $\dfrac{6}{5}$ b. $\dfrac{7}{24}$ c. $\dfrac{29}{24}$ d. $\dfrac{13}{24}$

42. Simplify: $\dfrac{5}{18} + \dfrac{2}{9} - \dfrac{1}{4}$

    a. $\dfrac{1}{3}$ b. $\dfrac{1}{4}$ c. $\dfrac{3}{4}$ d. $\dfrac{1}{6}$

43. Subtract: $6\dfrac{2}{3} - 3\dfrac{7}{8}$

    a. $3\dfrac{5}{24}$ b. $3\dfrac{19}{24}$ c. $2\dfrac{19}{24}$ d. $2\dfrac{3}{8}$

44. Add: $12\frac{3}{8} + 2\frac{1}{4}$

   a. $14\frac{2}{7}$ b. $14\frac{5}{8}$ c. $14\frac{3}{28}$ d. $14\frac{5}{8}$

45. Subtract: $24 - 4\frac{2}{3}$

   a. $20\frac{2}{3}$ b. $20\frac{1}{3}$ c. $28\frac{2}{3}$ d. $19\frac{1}{3}$

46. Simplify: $\frac{1}{2} + \frac{3}{4} - \frac{5}{6}$

   a. $2\frac{1}{12}$ b. $\frac{5}{12}$ c. $\frac{3}{4}$ d. $\frac{5}{6}$

47. Subtract: $7\frac{7}{12} - \frac{5}{8}$

   a. $6\frac{23}{24}$ b. $7\frac{23}{24}$ c. $6\frac{7}{12}$ d. $7\frac{7}{12}$

48. Multiply: $4\frac{2}{7} \bullet \frac{14}{15}$

   a. $\frac{1}{4}$ b. 4 c. $\frac{2}{3}$ d. $4\frac{2}{15}$

49. Multiply: $\frac{7}{8} \div 8$

   a. 7 b. $8\frac{7}{8}$ c. $\frac{7}{64}$ d. $\frac{1}{7}$

50. Divide: $2\frac{1}{4} \div 12$

   a. $\frac{1}{16}$ b. 27 c. 21 d. $\frac{3}{16}$

51. Simplify: $\left(\frac{2}{3} + \frac{5}{6}\right) \div \frac{5}{9}$

   a. $\frac{5}{6}$ b. $2\frac{7}{10}$ c. $\frac{3}{10}$ d. $\frac{7}{5}$

52. Simplify: $\frac{5}{6}\left(\frac{2}{3}-\frac{1}{6}\right)+\frac{3}{4}$

   a. $1\frac{1}{24}$ b. $\frac{1}{2}$ c. $1\frac{1}{6}$ d. $1\frac{7}{12}$

53. What is 12% of 60?
   a. 720   b. 72   c. 0.72   d. 7.2

54. What is 1.5 percent of 80?
   a. 1.2   b. 1.875   c. 18.75   d. 120

55. 22 is 220% of what?
   a. 10   b. 22   c. 484   d. 100

56. A plane travels 2047.5 miles in 3.5 hours. Find the plane's speed in miles per hour.
   a. 7166.25 mph   b. 585 mph   c. 0.0004885 mph   d. 5850 mph

57. A shoe store has a pair of leather boots on sale for $89.60, which is 80% of the original price. What was the original price?
   a. $112   b. $22.40   c. $71.68   d. $100

58. Your salary is now $24,000 and you expect a 7.5% raise in salary next year. What will be your new salary?
   a. $42,000   b. $1,800   c. $25,680   d. $25,800

59. Your salary is $40,000 and you receive a raise of $2400. What percent of your salary is your raise?
   a. 6%   b. 0.06%   c. 16%   d. 0.016%

60. You've just received a 3.5% salary increase of $1085 per year. What was your original salary?
   a. $37.98   b. $3100   c. $31,000   d. $32,085

61. A home was sold for $250,000. This was 125% of the original cost. What was the original cost of the home?
   a. $200,000   b. $225,000   c. $312,500   d. $3,125,000

62. Dan's test scores for the semester were 85, 96, 78, 88, and 92. What was the mean for the 5 tests?
   a. 88   b. 78   c. 87.8   d. 73

63. Fifteen students in my math class are also taking French. If this is 30% of the class, how many students are in the class?

    a. 35   b. 50   c. 15   d. 40

64. A new box of corn flakes contains 22 ounces of cereal. How many $2\frac{3}{4}$ ounce portions can be served from this box?

    a. 60.5   b. 8   c. 9   d. 7

65. For every 40 pounds of body weight, the dosage for a medication is $\frac{1}{2}$ ounce. If a person weighs 180 pounds, how many ounces of medication should be given?

    a. 1oz.   b. 2oz   c. 2.5oz   d. 2.25oz

66. The number of students enrolled in Math Skills I increased from 1500 to 1800 during the first week of registration. What was the percent increase?

    a. 120%   b. 20%   c. 200%   d. 12%

67. A college would like to increase its current enrollment by 5.5%. What will the total number of students be after the increase if the original enrollment was 16,000 students?

    a. 880   b. 16,880   c. 8800   d. 1688

68. A new car cost $30,000 and after a year it depreciated and it is now worth $22,500. What is the percent decrease?

    a. 2.5%   b. 75%   c. 25%   d.7.5%

69. A store uses a 35% markup rate. What is the selling price of a refrigerator that was purchased by the store for $800?

    a. $280   b. $1080   c. $1360   d. $936

70. A manufacturer employs 1200 people during the holiday season. At the end of the season the company decreased the number of its employees to 720 employees. What was the percent decrease?

    a. 40%   b. 4%   c. 60%   d. 6%

Use the following set of numbers for problems #71, #72, #73:
11, 12, 15, 12, 17, 13

71. Find the mean: (*Round to nearest tenth of percent*)

    a. 12.5   b. 16   c. 13.3   d. 80

72. Find the median:

    a. 13   b. 12   c. 12.5   d. 16

73. Find the mode:
    a. 16   b. 12   c. 12.5   d. 13

74. Complete the following: 8 gallons = _____quarts
    a. 2   b. 32   c. 48   d. 4

75. Complete the following: 500 cm = _____meters
    a. 5000   b. 0.5   c. 5   d. 50

76. Complete the following: 108 in = _____yards
    a. 9   b. 6   c. 4   d. 3

For problems #77 and #78, use the following pie chart showing an employee's weekly income of $425:

Take Home Pay 56%

Federal Tax 28%

State Tax 6%   Savings 10%

77. Find the amount taken out for federal and state taxes.
    a. $144.50   b. $119.00   c. $22.50   d. $246.50

78. Find the amount that the employee takes home.
    a. 42.50   b. $425.00   c. $382.50   d. $238.00

79. Find the area of the following figure:

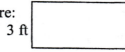

3 ft

5.5ft

    a. $8.5ft^2$ b. $16.5 ft^2$ c. 16.5ft   d. $20ft^2$

80. Find the length of a fence needed to enclose the yard shown in the figure :

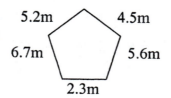

5.2m   4.5m
6.7m   5.6m
2.3m

    a. 21.3m   b. 23.4m   c. 24.3m   d. 25.4m

81. Find the area of a square whose sides are 5.3 yards.
    a. 21.2 yds^2 b. 25.3 yds^2 c. 28.09 yds^2 d. 28.99 yds^2

82. Find the circumference of a circle with radius 18 inches. *(Round to nearest inch)*
    a. 36 in   b. 56 in   c. 72 in   d. 113 in

83. Find the perimeter of the triangle:

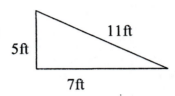

      a. 23 ft   b. 35 ft   c. 77 ft   d. 385 ft

84. Find the area of a circle with a diameter of 6 inches. (Use 3.14 for π)
    a. 113.04 in^2 b. 28.26 in^2 c. 18.84 in^2 d. 9.42 in^2

85. Find the perimeter of a triangle with sides 1.5 in, 2 in, $2\frac{3}{4}$ in.

      a. 8.25 in   b. 6.25 in   c. 4.13 in   d. 4.45 in

86. Find the area of a triangle with a base of 14 ft and a height of 14 ft.
    a. 196 ft^2 b. 28 ft^2 c. 42 ft^2 d. 98 ft^2

87. Complete the following: 25 °C = _____°F
    a. 77   b. 13   c. 50   d. 57

88. Complete the following: 14m = _____mm
    a. 14,000   b. 140   c. 0.014   d. 0.00014

89. Complete the following: 105 lbs = ____kg
    a. 472.5   b. 233.33   c. 231   d. 47.25

90. Complete the following: 56 oz = _____g
    a. 2   b. 25.2   c. 123.2   d. 1568

91. Complete the following: 212 °F = ____°C
    a. 100   b. 0   c. 180   d. 32

92. Complete the following: 5 °C = _____°F
    a. 15   b. 41   c. 15.4   d. 32

Answers to Comprehensive Review

1. c	15. b	29. a	43. c	57. a	71. c	85. b
2. c	16. b	30. d	44. d	58. d	72. c	86. d
3. b	17. c	31. b	45. d	59. a	73. b	87. a
4. d	18. a	32. a	46. b	60. c	74. b	88. a
5. d	19. a	33. d	47. a	61. a	75. c	89. d
6. a	20. d	34. c	48. b	62. c	76. d	90. d
7. c	21. c	35. a	49. c	63. b	77. a	91. a
8. d	22. c	36. b	50. d	64. b	78. d	92. b
9. d	23. a	37. c	51. b	65. d	79. b	
10. a	24. b	38. d	52. c	66. b	80. c	
11. c	25. b	39. b	53. d	67. b	81. c	
12. a	26. c	40. a	54. a	68. c	82. d	
13. c	27. a	41. d	55. a	69. b	83. a	
14. d	28. b	42. b	56. b	70. a	84. b	

Math Fundamentals Review

Appendix

Conversion Chart

English Measurement

Length		Weight	
1 foot (ft)	= 12 inches (in)	1 pound (lb)	= 16 ounces (oz)
1 yard (yd)	= 3 feet (ft)	1 ton (T)	= 2000 pounds (lb)
1 mile (mi)	= 5280 feet (ft)		
Capacity		**Time**	
1 cup (c)	= 8 fluid ounces(fl oz)	1 week (wk)	= 7 days
1 pint (pt)	= 2 cups(c)	1 day	= 24 hours (hr)
1 quart (qt)	= 2 pints (pt)	1 hour (hr)	= 60 minutes (min)
1 gallon (gal)	= 4 quarts (qt)	1 minute (min)	= 60 seconds (sec)
1 pint (pt)	= 16 fluid ounces (fl oz)		

Metric Measurement

100 cm	= 1 m	1000 g = 1 kg
1000 mm	= 1 m	1000 mg = 1g
1000 m	= 1 km	1000 kg = 1 metric ton
10 mm	= 1 cm	
1 *deka*meter (dam) = 10m		1000mL = 1 L
1 *hecto*meter (hm) = 100m		
1 *kilo*meter (km) = 1000m		

kilo   hecto   deka   <u>BASE</u>   deci   centi   milli

grams

Liters

meters

Metric & English

Metric to English		English to Metric	
1 kilometer	≈ 0.62 mile	1 mile	≈ 1.6 kilometers
1 cm	≈ 0.394 in	1 yard	≈ 0.914 meter
1 meter	≈ 3.28 feet	1 foot	≈ 0.30 meter
1 meter	≈ 1.09 yards	1 inch	≈ 2.54 centimeters
1 centimeter	≈ 0.39 inch		
1 meter	≈ 39.37 in	1 gallon	≈ 3.78 liters
		1 quart	≈ 0.95 liter
1 liter	≈ 0.26 gallon		
1 liter	≈ 1.06 quarts	1 pound	≈ 0.45 kilogram
		1 ounce	≈ 28 grams
1 kilogram	≈ 2.2 pounds		
1 gram	≈ 0.035 ounce		

Temperature Conversion

$C = \dfrac{5(F-32)}{9}$	$F = \dfrac{9 \bullet C}{5} + 32$

Geometry Formulas

Area	Perimeter
$A_{\square} = lw$	$P_{\square} = 2L + 2W$
$A_{\triangle} = \frac{1}{2}bh$	$P_{\triangle} = $ The sum of all sides
$A_{\odot} = \pi r^2$	$C_{\odot} = \pi d$ or $C_{\odot} = 2\pi r$

$D_{\odot} = 2r$ Diameter of a Circle = Twice the radius	$R_{\odot} = \frac{1}{2}D$ Radius of a Circle = $\frac{1}{2}$ the Diameter

All points on the circumference of a circle are equidistant from its center.